STOP FIGHTING

and START

COMMUNICATING

STOP FIGHTING

and START COMMUNICATING

BY

DAPHNA LEVY

Golden MILLENNIUM productions PUBLISHING

Stop Fighting and Start Communicating
by Daphna Levy

www.MarriageAide.com

Published by Golden Millennium Productions, Inc.
www.GoldenProductions.com

Paperback ISBN: 978-1-886668-95-9
Paperback first edition 2024
Printed in the United States of America

Edited by Janet K. Stephens
Cover design, interior design and illustrations by Art-&-Design Plus

Library of Congress Cataloging-in-Publication Data

Name: Daphna Levy
Title: Stop Fighting and Start Communicating / Daphna Levy
Description: Golden Millennium Publishing paperback edition 2024
Identifiers: LCCN 2023914031 | ISBN 978-1-886668-95-9
Subjects: NONFICTION / Relationships. Love. Marriage. Communication. Stop fighting.

CONTENTS

Dedication IX

Introduction XI

Chapter 1 | How Communication Goes Wrong 1

Chapter 2 | Timing Is Everything 5
  Two Aspects of Timing 9
  Can We Ever Talk? 11
  Finding the Right Time 11

Chapter 3 | The Power Struggle 15

Chapter 4 | Avoid These Pitfalls 19
  Twists and Turn 19
  Do You Assume? 21
  Body Language 23
  Tone 25

Chapter 5 | The Garden of Love 31
  When Did You Stop Selling? 32
  The Selling Must Go On 33
  The Way You Were 34
  Courtship 36
  Your Family 37

Chapter 6 | Toxic Influences 43
    People 44
    Movies and TV 46
    Social Media 47
    Phones 48
    How You Spend Your Time 49
    Keep It Positive 50

Chapter 7 | The Enemy Within 53
    Criticism Is Toxic 53
    Water the Flowers, Not the Weeds 54
    Disrespect 56
    Dishonesty 57
    Lack of Support 60
    Don't Ruin It! 61

Chapter 8 | Sex and Your Happiness 67
    Foreplay 68
    Helicopters vs. Airliners 69
    How Sex Life Deteriorates 70
    Other Reasons 71
    The Grass Is Greener
    Where You Water It 72

Chapter 9 | Settling Your Differences 77
    Horses vs. Mules 77
    Attitude Is Everything 78
    Your Goals 80
    How to Stay in Harmony 82
    Balancing Your Communication 85

Multitasking   87
Affection   88
Drive   89
What a Mess!   91

Chapter   10| Let Them Be   95

Chapter   11| Children, Blended Families
                and Co-Parenting   101
                Should You Be Your Child's Friend?   101
                The Power of Quality Time   102
                The Secret to Good Behavior   104
                Do the Kids Come Between You?   106
                Blended Families   108
                Co-Parenting   109
                The Curse Called "Devices"   110
                The Truth about ADHD   113
                Autism Spectrum Disorder   116

Chapter   12| Start Communicating!   121
                They Don't Listen   122
                Eye Contact   123
                Copy That   124

Smart Relationship Analysis™ | Couples' Quiz   129
                Instructions   130

Index   195

DEDICATION

To all couples out there who love each other dearly,
yet struggle to communicate.

INTRODUCTION

"We can't communicate. We fight and argue all the time, over the smallest things!" This is the most common complaint I hear from couples.

Whether the fighting is over significant issues such as infidelity, parenting or finance, or matters as minor as taking out the trash—if you are fighting, you have long since stopped communicating.

When a simple discussion gets out of hand, it escalates and becomes an argument. Once an argument gets heated, it turns into a fight. During arguments and fights people stop listening. They talk over each other, sling accusations, even exchange swear words. Emotions run high and any willingness to try and understand each other goes out the window.

Arguments and fights tear apart relationships and have ended many marriages. Homelife becomes unbearable. Children are deprived of the security and stability they need and deserve. To the couple, those fights bring great pain and wear away at the love they once shared.

I've been told, "We need to learn how to fight correctly." There is no such thing as "correct fighting" any more than there are "wonderful wars." People get hurt and die in war, both winners and losers.

Similarly, no one wins an argument or a fight. You might prove your point and "be right" but at what cost? You have lost some of your partner's affections and earned more of their resentment. Your harmony has been disrupted and now you can't communicate at all.

What happened?

1   You were having a conversation.

2 Your conversation went off the rails and turned into an argument.

3 Then the argument got out of control, and you found yourselves fighting.

Clearly, had you been able to stay at the conversation level, you would never have fought or even argued. Only when conversations fail, do situations escalate and reach the stage of arguing and then fighting.

Fortunately, it is possible to learn how to communicate effectively, and have real conversations and fruitful discussions, even about difficult issues. And if you can do so, you will never have to wonder how to "fight correctly."

How Communication Goes Wrong

Chapter 1 | *How Communication Goes Wrong*

When people start a new relationship, their communication is usually pretty good. They show interest in each other's stories, feelings and thoughts. They listen attentively and talk to each other lovingly, or at least respectfully. After all, they are still trying to earn each other's love. So, they are on their best behavior and do their best to get along. After some time, they get comfortable and stop putting in the work. That's when arguments and fights begin.

In my offices, we receive many cries for help like this one:

"My husband and I have been arguing a lot. We're not good at communicating with each other anymore. We're losing respect for each other, so the fights have been getting progressively worse. We both end up saying things we don't mean and threatening each other with divorce."

Most arguments start with minor issues. You don't get up in the morning and bring up your deepest feelings, or spend dinnertime after a long day of work discussing major life decisions. Instead, arguments start with comments about dishes, taking out the trash or folding laundry.

In my office, I often hear, "We had a big fight this week." Then the couple look at each other trying to recall what the fight was about. It was that minor! Still, it escalated, became an argument and made them angry and upset at each other. Some couples even stop talking for several days or weeks.

We can all talk. But can we communicate?

Politicians can talk. Drunks can talk. But do they communicate? Do they make themselves understood? Do they listen? Do they hear you, or are they too busy preparing their own rebuttal? Are they even interested in understanding your point of view?

Good communication skills are vital to any relationship. Yet they are seldom seen. They are not taught at school and examples of them in life are rare to nonexistent. Perhaps you have witnessed your parents fighting and arguing or—in later years—heard the loud silence that marked their disconnection. You have participated in groups where no one listened, people interrupted each other mid-sentence and the loudest person took over the conversation. And you may have gone on dates where the other person talked nonstop, believing they were "a great communicator."

Any couple who lacks communication skills should expect most discussions to turn into arguments or fights.

There are many reasons why communication goes wrong. The following chapters explain the most common of them and provide the tools couples need to stop fighting and start communicating.

Chapter 2

*Timing
Is Everything*

Chapter 2 | *Timing Is Everything*

If you have your own children or other people's children in your life, or if you have ever observed a baby or young child, you know that tired or hungry children are not the same sweet things they can be when they are well fed and rested. To be perfectly honest, we adults are not much different. We can get "hangry" when hungry, and moody when tired.

Those conditions and several others practically guarantee an argument, no matter how minor the topic of discussion, as in the following example.

A husband comes home at night. He's been up since 5:00 a.m. and he's had nothing to eat since lunch. He has a headache and is worried about a situation at work. Now the kids want his attention. After all, they haven't seen him all day and have a lot to tell him…

His wife had broken sleep the night before because the baby was teething. Since returning home from work, she's been with the kids —not a moment to herself. She is cooking dinner. She's as hungry as everyone else. It's chaotic and everybody seems to have a short fuse.

Under such circumstances, communication goes wrong. Partners get irritable and short-tempered. They say hurtful words they later regret but cannot take back. And any conversation quickly turns into an argument.

Hunger, tiredness, physical pain, being ill or under the weather; being stressed or having attention on some worry or concern—any of these factors could turn a simple conversation into an argument or fight.

The following story, told to me by a client, illustrates what could happen when a discussion takes place at the ***wrong time***.

"It was late at night and a disagreement came up," my client explained. "My husband reminded me of your advice, to avoid late-night discussions, but I insisted. I wanted to resolve the matter right there and then.

"So we stood outside the house to avoid waking the children and argued for an hour. Finally, we went to bed angry and exhausted, with no resolution."

"The next morning," she continued, "we talked about it over breakfast and resolved the entire issue in five minutes!"

That's the difference between right and wrong timing.

Another factor that deeply affects a couple's ability to communicate is the use of drugs, including alcohol. (Yes, alcohol is a drug.) I have worked with couples who have had huge fights whenever they had been drinking, even a little. When alcohol was involved, they did not have to be drunk for conversations to get off the rails and turn into fights.

It isn't uncommon for couples to show up at my office after a weekend of celebration, licking their wounds from arguments they wouldn't have had while completely sober. Alcohol can have such an effect, even if people are not drunk.

Let's put alcohol and other drugs in perspective. Suppose you planned a trip overseas. You would be flying over the Atlantic Ocean with your entire family, children and all—the people nearest and dearest to your heart. Would you let the pilot have a beer, take a shot or smoke a joint before takeoff? Would you feel safe putting your life and your family's life in that person's hands?

That's how "safe" your communication is when either one of you is under the influence, to any degree.

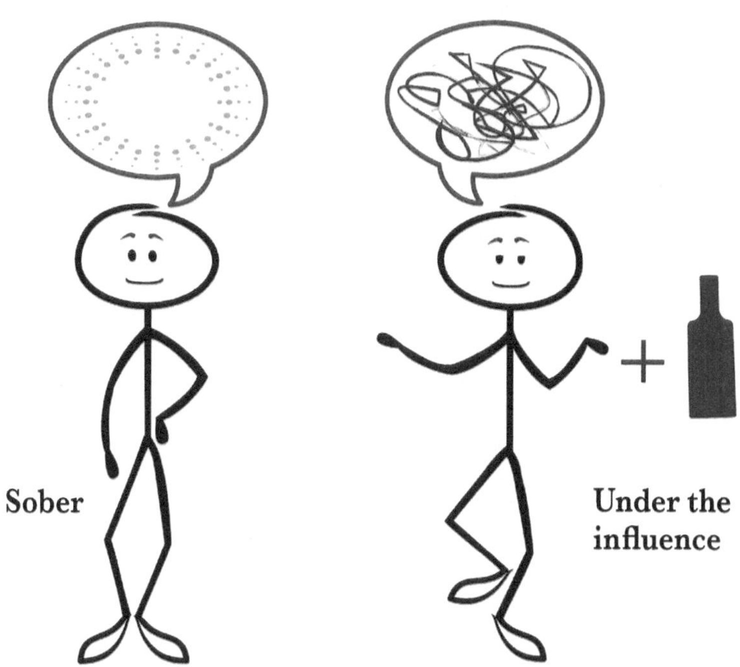

Another reason communication goes wrong is having insufficient time for a full discussion. Even though you have something on your mind that you really need to discuss, one or both of you is in a hurry.

A client who was a police officer once said to his wife, "We need to talk." Only he did so a few short minutes before leaving for work. The poor wife spent an entire day wondering if he wanted a divorce.

When he returned home that night, she found out that it was nothing of the sort; just an ordinary family matter. Had he waited to bring it up when they had sufficient time for discussion, he would have saved her a day of agony.

So, before you start a meaningful conversation, make sure that neither one of you has to rush out the door or have dinner ready for company that's about to arrive, or has a deadline for a project, or an upcoming exam.

In summary, keep in mind the following conditions, which practically guarantee you bad communication, arguments or fights that could be avoided.

- Tiredness: lack of sleep, long days, late nights,

- Hunger: haven't eaten, skipped meals, ate junk,

- Alcohol and other drugs—any amount,

- Withdrawal symptoms due to stopping or reducing drug, alcohol or medication intake,

- Unwell condition: illness, aches and pains,

- PMS and other hormonal changes in women; taking steroids or testosterone (resulting in aggression) in men,

- Worry, stress, sadness; preoccupation with some problem or concern,

- In a hurry: not enough time for a proper discussion.

Save conversations for later if...

Two Aspects of Timing

Now you have your list. You know right timing from wrong. How can you use that to stop fighting and start communicating? Your strategy is twofold:

1) Observe your partner

You look at your partner and suspect that he or she may be hungry, tired, in pain, or worried. They, or perhaps both of you, are in a rush or have had a drink.

The thing to do is not take to heart anything he or she says. Ignore any rude comments or snappy reactions. Save discussions for later, when your partner is in better shape.

Now is the time to take care of him or her. Feed them, rub their back, take care of the children so they can take a shower, maybe send them to bed—whatever will help them recover.

And do not be offended if they do not thank you on the spot. You will be appreciated and may even get an apology for their rude behavior later on. You are setting a good example and hopefully, they will treat you with the same understanding when you need help and support.

2) **Observe yourself**

If you feel irritable, have a short fuse, become furious or easily offended; if you are stressed, anxious, sensitive, sad or on the verge of tears, it's time for a self-check. Not that life does not offer plenty of reasons to feel this way, but before you take yourself too seriously, make sure that your response to your partner is not intensified by your physical state and other circumstances.

Observe your own condition: are you tired, hungry, in pain, etc.? Have you had a rough day, received bad news or do you have some worry on your mind? Are you pressed for time? If you are a woman, is this your time of the month?

If so, do not take it out on your partner (or children!). Disregard any negative thoughts you have. This is not the time to draw conclusions or make life-altering decisions. Realize that your outlook on life is clouded by your physical condition or current circumstances.

Now is the time to take care of yourself. Feed your body or put yourself to bed. If possible, take a walk to distract your mind from your worries, frustration, or sadness. If you have been drinking, wait until you sober up fully to avoid lashing out or saying something you will later regret.

You could mention to your partner that you are hungry, tired, have had a rough day, or whatever else may be going on with you. Make sure he or she understands that it is not their fault and, if possible, get them to help and support you.

As can be seen, this process goes both ways: you observe your partner's condition and give him or her grace just as you would to a cranky baby; and you conduct a self-check of your own physical and emotional state, and give *yourself* grace.

If you can see that one or both of you are not in good condition (and therefore, temporarily, not in your right minds), do not attempt deep conversations or try to resolve serious matters.

Can We Ever Talk?

So, you ask, when do we ever get to talk and say what's on our minds? Life is a busy affair filled with work and career challenges, children, family and a bucketful of obligations.

True. Busy couples do not get to enjoy many sweet moments together like they did when they were dating. Instead, they struggle to find any quality time for intimate conversation.

You may have things on your mind, such as something your partner said or did that offended you or hurt your feelings, or some information you saw on his or her phone that concerned you; or you may simply wish to discuss your plans for the future.

Finding the Right Time

Try this: write down a list of the issues you wish to discuss with your partner. Time the conversation correctly. Make sure you are both well rested, fed, sober, etc. A quiet breakfast following a good night's sleep, or an alcohol-free lunch, might be ideal. Put your phones away and make sure you have enough time. That's when you bring up the issues on your list (one at a time, please) and have good communication about each.

Important matters should not be discussed over the phone if you can at all help it, and definitely not via text. While any communication that is not in person is challenging (you are unable to see facial expressions or make eye contact) "talking" over text is asking for trouble.

Text is dry. You cannot hear each other's tone, and whatever is said is easily misinterpreted. Many couples argue and fight via text. By the time they meet again, they are more upset with one another than they were when they last said goodbye.

So, make your list of issues and find the right time to discuss each until each one is resolved to your full satisfaction.

Timing is everything!

Chapter 3

The Power Struggle

Chapter 3 | *The Power Struggle*

The couple sitting in front of me were tired of years of arguing. They wanted to stop fighting and start communicating. "He's always right," the wife said. "He can never admit that he's wrong. It's his way or the highway." In response, she would defend herself and try to show him that she was right and he was wrong. They would argue and fight. It was an endless **power struggle**, an ongoing competition that nobody won.

The **power struggle** is a destructive habit that many couples have. They point fingers at each other. They argue about who did or didn't help or…who helped more. They fight over any issue, big or small, important or not. And, if one of them did something to offend the other, there is payback: "you've hurt me, I'll hurt you; … I won't support you."

None of the tools provided in this book are of use as long as this continues.

What such couples are missing is this: In a relationship, it makes no difference who is right or who gets his or her way. You can be "right" all the way to divorce court, so why bother?

What matters is being each other's friend and helping one another be better, happier, more successful people because you are together. The following real-life story is an example of that.

Christine and David were a couple in constant competition with one another. They argued daily, on a variety of subjects.

As parents in a blended family, he defended his son's laziness in the face of her criticism while she defended her son's reputation to him. If his son did something wrong, he would "prove" to her that her son did worse, and vice versa. There were other topics for argument such as household chores, bills, and whether or not they should hold hands in public.

Their relationship took a significant turn for the better when they took my advice and agreed to stop the competition. "Instead of competing against each other," I said, "turn your energy toward life and start working together as a team to overcome the daily challenges that life presents you as individuals, as a couple and as a family."

They did. I had never seen them happier! The arguments ceased and they started to have good communication, probably for the first time in years.

Never forget that your relationship should be, first and foremost, a friendship. You are life partners, and partners should cooperate with each other, help one another, and act as a team.

If the members of a sports team competed among themselves, they would fail to defeat their true opponent —the opposing team. In life, your "opponents" are the challenges you face daily: physically, emotionally, financially, professionally and on and on. Those are your enemies, not your partner.

So be a team—a good team—and that will make both of you winners. Working together—not against each other —you can create happiness and success for you as individuals, as a couple and a family.

> ***Now we aren't fighting like we are on trial for death row.***
>
> —Freddy, Client

Chapter 4

*Avoid
These Pitfalls*

Chapter 4 | *Avoid These Pitfalls*

Wrong timing is a significant pitfall on your road to good communication and so is the power struggle. But there are additional traps that, in the heat of the moment, are easy to fall into, and before you know it, they involve you in an argument. Your best intentions to have a good conversation or spend a nice day together fail. You look back and can hardly tell how it all went wrong, but it's too late. You are upset with one another and remain so for hours and sometimes days.

Fortunately, recognizing the following pitfalls will help you avoid them and the arguments they bring.

Twists and Turns

Have you ever started a discussion about topic A and before you knew it, it veered onto topic B then C and D? The communication twisted and turned and suddenly you found yourself arguing. For instance:

He: *"Why does it take you so long to get ready? We're going to be late."*

She: *"Because you never help me."*

He: *"I don't help? Your son never helps! And you don't know how to discipline him."*

She: *"You never liked my son."*

He: *"And you always complain about my daughter."*

She: *"That's because she is just like her mother."*

He: *"What's your problem with my ex?"*

She: *"Stop defending your ex! She has caused us enough trouble already."*

He: *"No! The real toxic person is your sister."*

And so on…

What happened? All they were trying to do was leave the house on time! But by deflecting and jumping from one topic to another, they became unable to reach a resolution on any of the issues that were brought up. Instead, they wound up with several open discussions and a long list of disagreements. That's a sure way to become even more upset with one another at the end of a conversation than before it began.

Jumping topics

In the previous example, trouble could have been avoided had she responded differently. When he said, "Why does it take you so long to get ready? We're going to be late," she could have given a real answer such as, "After I dressed the baby, he went again. So I had to change his diaper."

But even if she was in the wrong and jumped topics (perhaps she was tired and irritable), he still had the power to stop the decline. When she snapped with, "Because you never help me," he could have been the bigger person, ignored her snappy response, and said, "What can I do to help now?" That would have kept them working as a team and the conversation would not have gone off the rails.

So, the thing to do is stay on topic and resist the temptation to throw "stuff" at your partner just because the opportunity has presented itself. If there are issues you need to work out, pick the right time and discuss them properly. That way, you will be able to reach a resolution rather than piling up disagreements as in the above example.

Do You Assume?

Assuming is another pitfall that turns minor issues into domestic battles. Many people, instead of trying to understand, assume that they do. Perhaps you tell your partner something—or vice versa—and he or she takes it the wrong way. You say A and they hear B. They say "apples" and you hear "pears." Next thing you know, you are arguing.

A conversation could go as follows:

She: *"I need more help around the house. I have such a hard time with the kids every night, and…"*

He: *"So, you're saying I don't help?*
     Only you work around here?"
     "You never see what I do! You don't appreciate me!"

Or,

He: *"I've had a lot of stress at work lately. I need some*
     alone time. You know, like when you take time to
     do your hair and nails…"

She: *"So now you want me to stop doing my hair and nails?*
     It's the only thing I do for myself. I work hard.
     I deserve it."

Here, a fight began because he assumed her "needing help around the house" really meant that "he never helps." Or because she assumed that his "needing some alone time" really meant that she should stop going to the salon.

Without making assumptions, these communications could go something like this:

She says that she needs help around the house and that she has a hard time with the kids at night. He listens well and hears, "My wife needs help around the house. She has a hard time with the kids at night." Now he might respond with,"I know what you mean. The kids are a handful. Let me help you get them to bed and let's spend some time relaxing together."

Similarly, when he says that he has had a lot of stress and needs some alone time, she should hear, "My husband is stressed and needs some time for himself." Her response might be, "I understand. We need to figure out how you can have some time for yourself. Let's talk about it after dinner and see what we can work out."

So, train yourself to listen to what you hear and take it in as it is. If he says, "I like my mother's stew..." you should not assume that he is saying "I don't like your cooking..." and explode with, "Then go eat at your mother's!"

Without assumptions, understanding is possible. With assumptions, misunderstandings are guaranteed, and those lead to arguments and fights. In the words of one of my clients:

We have a greater ability to communicate what we need from each other rather than assume and make the wrong assumption.

—Client

But misunderstanding of the words being said is not the only reason communication goes wrong. There are other aspects of communication that could be misunderstood, so read on.

Body Language

Just as people could misunderstand what they hear, so could they misconstrue what they see: their partner's body position, facial expressions, physical movement or even silence—what is commonly known as "body language."

Crossing one's arms over one's chest is one example. Some "experts" claim that crossed arms mean the person is angry, defensive, tense, distant, arrogant and such. These are all assumptions, of course. Someone invented a definition for that body position as if it were a word in the dictionary.

The following real-life story is an example.

I had just helped one of my couples resolve a disagreement. However, because the husband was sitting there with his arms crossed, the wife was convinced that he was still upset.

I'm not upset" he said, "but sitting in this chair I have no place to rest my arms, so I'm crossing them over my chest."

Clearly, his body language seemed to his wife to say something he did not say, think or feel. The following real-life story is another example.

Jasmine and Tony arrived at my office upset with each other. On the drive over, a discussion of a minor issue had turned into an argument. So we talked about it and worked out a solution that would prevent similar conversations from getting out of hand in the future.

Jasmine was very pleased and felt that the new tools I had just given them would serve them well in the future. She was relieved, but was still deep in thought, processing it all.

Tony, still feeling wounded from the argument that had ruined their morning, took one look at her and said,

"You're still upset!"

"No," she said, "I'm not. This is a perfect solution."

"Yes, you are," he insisted, "I can see it."

"No, I'm not!"

Fortunately, I was there to referee, or this would have turned into into a new argument.

Couples tend to be overly sensitive to each other's responses. If one partner seems thoughtful or quiet at the conclusion of an argument, as in the examples above, the other might misread their body language and assume something is wrong. A new argument could develop.

Clearly, body language is wide open to interpretation and could lead to misunderstandings. A person may frown because of concentration, thoughtfulness, or physical discomfort. Do not assume that there is a problem between that person and you. They may laugh at something they have seen or heard. Do not assume that they are laughing at you.

Instead of telling them how they feel or what they think based on their body language, ask them. Only then can you be sure that your interpretation is correct.

Tone

Tone can make or break a communication. How you and your partner sound could make the difference between a successful conversation and the start of a fight. You may ask for a cup of coffee politely or in a commanding tone of voice. You may say "thank you" lovingly or angrily. People are sensitive to tone, and many arguments start, not because of what was said, but how it was said.

Let's say the wife asks her husband to fix a leak in the kitchen faucet. She sounds annoyed, resentful, critical. While her words convey her request, her tone expresses her frustration, as if to say, "How many more times do I have to ask you to do this?!" He reacts to the tone, not the words, and an argument ensues.

I have found that, just as the **wrong tone** may lead to an argument, the **right tone** may allow you to express almost anything without creating a conflict or making an enemy out of the person to whom you are talking.

I was in my office, expecting my next couple. The wife walked in alone. "Where is Joe?" I asked.

"He's in the car smoking a joint... Don't tell him I told you."

"Oh, I will," I replied, and stepped out to greet the husband.

Joe was a habitual marijuana user of many years and had no desire to stop. The drug was his way of escaping his problems. I had accepted them for a short coaching program to see if I could help save their marriage.

Teaching drug users and alcoholics the tools of relationships is challenging, as their behavior constantly changes with the effects of the substance. They are not in control. However, these were good people and had young children. I was willing to give them a chance. I met Joe outside the office door. I looked straight at him and said softly, "What are you doing? I'm trying to help you save your marriage and keep your family together. You've told me that you cry every night because you're away from your kids. It's bad enough that you smoke all day, every day, but now you come to my office high as a kite? How am I supposed to help you? And besides, you stink. Don't come to my office smelling like this."

He nodded in agreement like a little boy who had been caught misbehaving. He was not upset with me. He knew I cared. I let him in and we proceeded to have our session.

That's the power of tone—the **right tone**.

Many couples use unacceptable tones with one another. They sound mean, uncaring, disrespectful or plain hostile. Some use cuss words. That's no way to treat your lover. I'll bet they did not use those tones, or vocabulary, when they were still working to earn their partner's love. If such tones were wrong then, what makes them right now?

When your tone conveys indifference, disapproval, anger, threat, blame, frustration, unfriendliness or hostility, the listener stops hearing your words. The tone takes over and masks the communication.

For example, when a parent says to a child, "I want you to be successful," their intentions are good. Perhaps they want to stop the child from making the same mistakes they themselves have made. They are trying to help. But the wrong tone of voice drowns the message and the child may hear, "You're a big disappointment."

Using a better tone permits you to communicate exactly what's on your mind without holding back, just as I did with my weed-smoking client.

Many couples hold back communication to avoid conflict. They are afraid that what they have to say will come out wrong and result in an argument. So instead of expressing their feelings or opinions, they let their frustrations build up. At last they explode, resulting in a bigger fight.

You need not hold back. Simply choose the **_right time_** (not tired, hungry, under the influence, etc.) and use the **_right tone_**.

Kindness usually wins, especially in relationships. That is not to say that your spouse could abuse you, cheat and lie while you respond with kindness. A divorce may be more appropriate. But in most cases, why not communicate pleasantly? After all, a relationship is supposed to be a loving connection.

If you put the right tone together with the right time, as described in an earlier chapter, you have a winning combination that could guarantee good communication instead of arguments and fights.

Chapter 5

The Garden of Love

Chapter 5 | *The Garden of Love*

A relationship is like a garden. You start a garden. You plant seedlings, flowers and young trees, then you care for them. You make sure to water them regularly, fertilize the ground and pull out the weeds. If a plant looks unhealthy, you try to help it. You do whatever it takes to keep your garden alive and "happy." That is how most couples start out and how they conduct themselves when they first meet.

They are attentive to each other's needs, as you are to your garden. They make efforts to listen, to be considerate and to make each other happy. They are on their best behavior and cherish every moment they spend together. At this stage of the relationship, each of them is still "selling" his or her partner on having a relationship, so they work hard to prove themselves.

Then they get married.

They turn on the automatic sprinklers and leave the garden to the mercy of nature. Sprinklers break down and some years there is drought. Yet they do not check their plants for health and happiness. Now they have a garden, they think, and they take it for granted. Won't it always be there?

No, the garden will not, and neither will the relationship. The following real-life story illustrates that.

When Betty and Jeff first came to my office, they had been separated for some months. A married couple and parents to three young children, they faced a dilemma. Betty had fallen in love with a coworker and had moved out. Jeff wanted her back, and she felt confused. While she wanted to keep her family together, she had feelings for the new man in her life.

Jeff told me their story: They were high school sweethearts who later married and started a family. As time went on, Jeff stopped showing Betty affection. He did not give her his attention, would never compliment her, and was not romantic. They didn't even hold hands, and sex was rare. "There were gaps in my marriage," he said, "and this guy came and filled the gaps I had left."

Jeff's neglect by no means justified Betty's infidelity. But it illustrates how dead a garden could become. Here were two good people who had put their relationship on autopilot. Like lazy gardeners, they had taken their **garden of love** for granted. They believed that it would take care of itself, but it wilted and died through neglect. Then Betty's infidelity came in like a bulldozer and flattened it so that it was never to be revived again.

When Did You Stop Selling?

Can you recall the "sales job" you did on each other when you first met?

Did you listen to her attentively? Did you treat him with respect? Did you bring her flowers? Did you make his favorite dish? Did you pay compliments to one another on your looks or good works? Were you supportive of each other's goals? Did you display affection? Did you pay attention? Did you make each other a priority?

Yes, you did all that, because you were still selling yourself and working to earn your partner's love. But once the selling was done and the "customer" was closed, you got comfortable and stopped trying.

The Selling Must Go On

In a relationship, the sales job must continue! Every day of your life you should be selling yourselves to each other by being the best partners you can be. Your connection, love and happiness depend on it.

Selling comes into play in one's personal life as well. You should always sell yourself on achieving your goals, being successful (whatever success means to you) and taking your life to the next level. When the going gets tough and the obstacles are too great, one requires self-motivating to build a good life. That is your personal sales job, on yourself.

It can be hard to do in this world, where good examples are few. It is easier to settle for less, like most people do, or to follow the poor examples we see on TV, in movies and the tabloids. To be happy, you must insist on creating a better life and happier relationships. And when you do so, you are swimming upstream, so to speak. You are in the minority, almost an oddball. That's a choice we all have to make: follow the herd, or carve our own path. I hope you do the latter.

In romantic relationships, not only do some couples stop selling themselves to their partners until they act and feel like roommates. Some even treat each other with disrespect and hostility and do the very things that bring pain into the relationship (infidelity ranking number one in pain and destruction). They become gardeners who rip up the flowers, kill the plants and chop down the trees.

What is the solution, you ask—how could this be fixed?

The Way You Were

The remedy is to go back to the way you were. By that I mean, go back to what you did and how you acted when you first started your *garden of love*.

How did you treat each other then?

What did you do that made your partner fall for you?

What did your partner do that made you fall in love with him or her?

If you had the answers to those questions, and if you reinstated your old, successful ways of tending your *garden of love*, you could rekindle your friendship, love and passion. You would once again treat each other in the way that brought you together in the first place and endeared you to one another. And your garden would once again flourish.

For instance, you may not be giving each other the attention you once did. Without attention, nothing grows: flowers, children, businesses, friendships, or love. Instead, you may be devoting your time and attention to social media or other people while neglecting each other. If you have ever neglected your plants, you know how deadly that can be.

Another factor may be affection. Some people are more affectionate than others, and people have different ways of expressing their affection. But affection cannot be omitted. You must give as much of it as your partner needs and ask to receive the amount you require.

If you have children, you know that one child may need more affection than another. If you want them to be happy, you are sensitive to their needs.

Karen and Richard shared the typical story of a couple who had let their garden wilt and nearly die. The children had grown and left the nest, and life became the typical routine of work, chores, and assisting family as needed. Richard couldn't see anything wrong with their life. They had a home and a successful business that provided all heir needs. But Karen, who had plenty on her plate with the house and the family, still missed the affection, attention and romance and felt unhappy.

One day she'd had enough. She checked herself into a hotel and that night she searched for help on the Internet. The next day they came to see me in my office.

I had them identify the actions and behavior that brought them happiness previously. For instance, early in their relationship, every morning before leaving for work Richard would leave Karen a gift card for a spa, a love note or some other treat next to her morning coffee. He would plan rides and short boating trips together. And there were other gestures that made her feel loved and special.

*These had all ceased and he started relying on the "automatic sprinklers." Realizing what had happened, Richard resumed his old successful actions and their **garden of love** started blooming again. In his testimonial, he wrote:*

We were able to get back to where we were forty years ago (sweethearts).

—Richard, Client

Courtship

Longman Dictionary defines courtship as "The period of time during which a man and woman have a romantic relationship before marrying." That includes the activities, effort and time invested to attract a partner and involve him or her romantically. Courtship starts the garden. But if you wish to keep it in bloom, you should never stop courting each other.

What Richard did was start courting Karen again. It was through that courtship that they rekindled their love and romance.

Courtship is as necessary to a mature relationship as it is when a relationship was young. It is as vital after the wedding as it is before marriage. Continuing to pursue each other provides the fertilizer, water, and gentle sunlight that nurture your *garden of love.* Always remember that wedding vows alone do not guarantee happiness or lasting love.

Never, never stop courting one another. Partners should express their love for each other continuously. It is not enough to say "I love you" once a year or to show your affection on special occasions. Would you expect a garden to thrive if you only watered it on birthdays and anniversaries?

Additionally, remember that the right tone plays a part in tending your garden of love or damaging it. Some people, instead of communicating calmly and pleasantly, bark out their communications. They raise their voices unnecessarily, lash out angrily, criticize, find fault, and are disrespectful. All that is not necessary for communication to take place. Most of the time, it prevents communication, because the person on the receiving end rejects it simply because of the aggressive tone.

An unpleasant tone alone starts arguments, and it wears away love and affection. I doubt that you used such tones with your partner during the "selling" phase.

Your Family

There is a lot that goes into raising a family. As duties and obligations increase, couples tend to neglect their *garden of love.* Such neglect comes at a price, because two or three decades later they feel like strangers. So never forget what started it all—the two of you.

Before there were children, there was you. And once your children leave the nest, there will once again be just the two of you.

You are the foundation of your family. You are the reason it came about. Nurture your *garden of love*. It is the world of just the two of you. Never stop tending it, while at the same time caring for your children, extended family, work, and life's many obligations.

If you take care of your *garden of love*, everyone will benefit in the long run. You will provide a safe, nurturing environment for your children. You will set a good example that gives the next generation hope for a happy marriage when they come of age. And, in this turbulent world, you will be living proof that the dream of a happy relationship can become reality.

then you grew.

Chapter 6

Toxic
Influences

Chapter 6 | *Toxic Influences*

The reason Heather and Jim came to see me was Jim's recent confession that he "didn't have feelings for her anymore." This came as a shock to Heather, because their five-year marriage seemed to be going just fine. The story went as follows:

Jim said that he was extremely bored in their routine-ridden marriage and that there was no love left in him. It looked as though I was faced with the challenge of trying to revive a dying or dead relationship.

So, I checked: Jim was not having an affair. He had not turned gay. He did not have any specific complaints about his wife, and he was not finding fault with her. Although he had dropped a bomb with his confession, he did not have his mind made up to get divorced. He had no clue what to do and neither did she.

I inquired further: Has anyone bad-mouthed Heather? Is there anyone in his life who is against her? Do his coworkers make fun of the idea of marriage or tell him he could do better? Is anyone flirting with him? Has he read anything that talked down relationships?

I kept asking until the enemy came to view.

It was a television show they watched regularly, which put relationships in a negative light. Like drops of poison, the negativity made its way into his mind and finally changed his feelings toward the woman he once loved. As our discussion continued and he recognized the toxic influence at its source, he became willing to work on the relationship.

As for the wife, she recognized that she had stopped nurturing their garden of love, leaving it to the mercy of the elements and the automatic sprinkler system. I guided them, and working together, they revived their relationship and rekindled their love.

Today more than ever, there are many ways negativity could creep into a relationship and poison it. You must be able to recognize the source of such negativity and keep it from affecting your relationship. As a couple, you are faced with enough challenges from within, as you are trying to get along and create your own happiness. Why let toxicity in from without?

Toxic Influences

If you take a good look at your life, you may recognize the toxic effects of some of the following sources and others similar to them.

People who talk negatively about your partner or about relationships, marriage, men or women in general. These may be parents or other close relatives, your boss or coworkers. They may be friends with whom you spend time and other people you trust, confide in, love and respect.

From now on, examine how you feel about your partner or your relationship after talking with one of those people. Do men or women seem bad to you? Are you not as happy to go home to your significant other? Do you secretly feel that your friend or friends are lucky to have their single life, or that their relationships are better than yours?

The following real-ife story is an example.

One young couple who came to see me were on the verge of divorce. After seven years together and the last three as a married couple, the wife decided that she did not want to be married anymore. She suddenly "fell out of love."

Just prior to that, she had started going out with her girlfriends. They would hop bars and get drunk. Looking at their lives, she felt like she had missed out on all the fun and it was time she started living life. The life she and her husband had built together, everything he had done for her in times of need and the opportunities she had to advance her life with him, lost their meaning. She was obsessed with her new, reckless life style.

I highly recommend that you never allow people who are dishonest, promiscuous, or immoral to affect the way you feel about your own relationship. It is guaranteed that they will have a negative effect on your life, so don't choose them as your role models.

I am reminded of a man who had repeatedly encouraged his son to seek extramarital affairs and would not rest until the son did. Crazy but true. That kind of influence is poison, and it may even come from someone you trust, love and respect, such as a parent.

This tells us that we must always maintain our right to judge anything we hear or see for ourselves. We must remain vigilant and not take things as gospel even if they seem to come from a reliable source. Every piece of information we get must be evaluated by each of us as to its truth and validity.

Never accept information blindly. In fact, I truly hope that as you read this book, you judge everything I say and determine whether it has truth, validity or usefulness to you and your relationship.

Movies and TV are loaded with negativity. There are stories of infidelity, embellished and glamorized. Watching them, you get the impression that "everybody" is unfaithful and that there is no honest soul left on the face of Earth.

The quality of movies has changed over the years. Decades ago, many films carried messages of high moral values, delivered hope, and showed that good could triumph over evil. They were uplifting. Nowadays, such positive movies are rare.

Instead, there are dating shows that put relationships in a terrible light and set an awful example for future generations to follow. Violence, alcohol, marijuana, and other drugs are glamorized. The people portrayed don't overcome life's hurdles naturally. Instead, there is a pill for everything, from sadness to worry, from loss to failure. And addiction itself is "cured" by new drugs. God help the parents who raise teenagers nowadays!

Movies and TV make people passive rather than proactive. That is why babies and children should not be seated in front of a TV or have a tablet or smartphone put in their hands. These may be good babysitters, but they dull their young minds and condition them to accept, rather than initiate. Success depends on initiative and drive.

Movies and TV programs have other, more immediate negative effects, as the following real-life story illustrates.

A newlywed young woman was fond of dating shows and other sensationalizing TV programs. By the time her husband came home at night, she would be worried and suspicious about who he had seen and what he might have done while away at work.

This young man was in love with his wife and busy building his business. He had no interest in looking outside the relationship.

However, she was so utterly poisoned by her favorite shows, that she refused to believe him. They got into bitter fights that destroyed the relationship and eventually led to divorce.

As you can see, negativity is all around us. It can poison our minds and damage our lives and relationships. And one way that it seeps into our world is through movies and TV.

That is not to say that you should never watch television or movies. But choose well, avoid negativity, and be aware of what is being presented to you. If you experience negative thoughts about your partner or family life, pause and detect some possible triggers: a movie, a show or a social media post?

And finally, do not spend so much time in front of the TV that you seldom communicate, because it is through communication that you will preserve your garden of love and create your happiness.

Social Media can be a significant source of toxicity and should be utilized wisely. The following real-life story is an example.

A client once called me, feeling down. It seemed like everyone she knew was doing better in life than she…at least according to their social media profiles. She felt like a failure.

I reminded her that people post their "happy front" on social media. They don't advertise their bad days, heartbreaks and disappointments. They may be crying themselves to sleep each night, but you won't see that in a post. She calmed down.

Social media creates false impressions, so take what you see with a grain of salt. There are images of people drinking and "having fun," but no pictures of the next day's hangover. There are pictures of couples embracing, but none show them fighting or sleeping in separate rooms. As with mainstream media, we are shown what someone wants you to believe, not what is really going on. The next real-life story is an example.

I was helping a client with his dating life. I never met the young lady he was hoping to date, only heard his stories of her.

She was physically unwell. She did not work, and an ex-boyfriend was paying the rent and other expenses in the hope of getting her back. She was severely depressed.

I was shocked to see her Instagram profile. She looked glamorous, successful and exuding confidence. Had I not heard the truth from my client, I could have been fooled.

So do not base your reality on social media. Do not let it set your standards for success and happiness, for right and wrong. And do not attempt to draw "wisdom" from memes and online videos. Maintain your own right to judge and evaluate everything that crosses your path.

Phones I hear a lot of complaints about people "being on their phones" when they should be mentally present with their spouse and family. Instead of communicating with the people who are physically there, they "talk" to people who are not, through text, social media, email and more.

Use your time wisely. Your children will not be little again. You will not always be their hero, and they will not always seek your company. Your partner and you have only so much time to spend together, so give each other attention and be there with him or her for real, and without distractions.

Lack of communication also affects sex life. You cannot be strangers all evening and expect intimacy at bedtime. Foreplay begins with "Hi honey. How was your day?" followed by listening and carrying on a conversation. That makes you feel connected and sets the tone for intimacy.

How You Spend Your Time

Time is precious. Once lost, it cannot be regained. Losing time is worse than losing money. You can always work to earn more money. Not so with time.

Life is busy with work, study, family and more. Most couples struggle to find time to be together, especially quality time that nurtures the relationship.

Phones, movies, television, electronic games, YouTube and social media are entertaining. So much so, that they are a magnet and a trap. They take you away from each other and affect the quality of your communication. You get too distracted to listen to each other or communicate effectively. And as a result, you are apart even when you are physically together. The following real-life story illustrates that.

A few years into their marriage, Sharon and Barry already felt disconnected. They did not make each other a priority and they let distractions like social media and YouTube consume their time and attention.

Realizing that, they agreed to put their phones away during dinner and before bedtime. They soon found that they got along better and deepened their connection. They started spending more time together and enjoying each other's company, as they used to before technology consumed their lives.

Keep It Positive!

Life is challenging. It is for that reason that we must eliminate toxic influences whenever and wherever possible and preserve our spirits for what's truly important.

Attitude has everything to do with happiness and success, and a positive attitude makes for a happier person who is able to meet life's challenges. So do not pollute your mind and heart with social toxicity. You need to stay positive in order to build your own future and help the people you love.

Chapter 7

The Enemy Within

Chapter 7 | *The Enemy Within*

The toxic influences your relationship faces from the outside are challenging enough. But nothing and no one has greater power to destroy your relationship than the two of you. By your own actions, intentional or unintentional, you could do so from within. The following real-life story is an example.

Jason adored his girlfriend and hoped to have her as his bride one day. It was during an argument that he started calling her names—pretty ugly ones too. What should have been a civilized discussion turned into a bad fight, revealing a mean side of him that she had not seen before.

Such behavior is common among couples. Here are two gardeners who should nurture their garden of love, but instead, they rip up the flowers and soak the soil with poison.

While you may be able to avoid outside negativity, if you act destructively in your own home, you will destroy your relationship from within.

Criticism Is Toxic

Anytime you criticize, condemn, and complain, you do damage to your ***garden of love*** and contribute to its destruction. It is not the type of behavior you want to adopt for daily living.

Some people tend to find fault in everything their partner does. They don't acknowledge the goodness that is there but look for faults. They carefully point out mistakes and tell them what's wrong with them: "You are a narcissist." "You are just like your mother." "You…" They seldom balance criticism of their partner by acknowledging that person's good works or virtues.

> *Any fool can criticize, condemn and*
> *complain—and most fools do.*
>
> —Benjamin Franklin

Water the Flowers, Not the Weeds

If you had two planters, one with flowers and the other with weeds, which would grow better? Obviously, the one you water.

Negativity and criticism are the weeds. Compliments, validation, recognizing the goodness in your partner—those are the flowers. Whichever you pay attention to will grow.

That is not to say that you should disregard dangerous weeds or sweep real issues under the rug. If your spouse comes home drunk, you would tackle the matter by choosing the right time and having a serious conversation aimed at putting an end to that behavior.

But so many of the disagreements couples have concern minor issues that are a matter of taste or opinion. Do not water those weeds. They will grow out of proportion to their actual importance. Focus on the positive. Even if your partner makes a mistake, was their intention good? Then water the intention, not the mistake. And give him or her a chance to correct it or do better next time.

The same is true of your own failures or mistakes—your personal weeds. If you dwell on them, you may become convinced that you can do nothing but fail. But if you welcome them as life lessons, you will be able to use the knowledge gained to do better in the future. And remember to pat yourself on the back for trying. Some people never do.

Water the flowers...

not the weeds.

Disrespect

Most people want to feel respected and appreciated. A relationship cannot thrive without mutual respect.

At times you may feel that there is nothing of value in your partner's personality—nothing to respect or appreciate. If so, why did you start a relationship with them in the first place? Have they completely changed, or do you choose to focus on their flaws and forget the good you originally saw in them?

Either way, disrespect is not the solution. It is extremely destructive, as the following real-life story illustrates.

Eric and Elizabeth sat in my office shouting at each other like bitter enemies. Each was telling the other how worthless, mean and ungrateful they were. Each was broadcasting their own good deeds at the top of their lungs. They were exchanging insults and using four-letter words.

It was hard to believe that this couple were once lovers who dreamed of raising a family and growing old together.

Partners tend to echo each other's tone and behavior. If one barks angrily, the other responds in kind. They go tit for tat. They play payback. They lose control of their emotions and say and do things they later regret, sometimes too late.

Just as anger begets anger and yelling begets yelling, patience, respect, and affection are likely to be responded to in kind. If they are not, find the right time and have a discussion. Remember not to assume but to hear what is actually being said. You will find that you are able to have a productive conversation and come up with solutions.

Suppose there is a disagreement about goals. She wants to go back to school to advance her career, earn more money, and have greater satisfaction in her work. Instead of understanding what she is actually saying, he assumes that she feels financially insecure and doubts his ability to provide or his commitment to the family. Perhaps he even fears that she may be preparing a Plan B in the event that the relationship doesn't work out. It is a sensitive subject and bringing it up results in arguments. She feels disrespected and unappreciated and so does he.

What they need to do is set aside time for conversation. It should be when they are not hungry, tired or ill; not over a glass of wine or under the influence; without distractions such as work, children, family or friends, TV, tablets or phones; not late at night, and with enough time for an in-depth discussion.

In such a conversation, with communication going back and forth, they would be able to convey their thoughts and feelings to each other. They would listen to one another with a sincere desire to understand and without assumptions. Each would feel like their point of view was heard and appreciated. Continuing the discussion in that manner they would eventually reach agreement. It could take more than one conversation, but they would be able to work things out and come up with a plan of action while maintaining mutual respect and good communication.

Dishonesty

I cannot stress enough how damaging dishonesty is to a relationship. Like any other partnership, a relationship requires mutual honesty and trust.

When people form business partnerships, they do not look forward to being swindled. Agreements must be kept and truth must shine. The moment that business or life partners start to lie to each other, hide information or in any way violate the trust put in them, the partnership starts to disintegrate.

In today's world, dishonesty and disloyalty are common, making us believe that those are acceptable standards. They are not. Additionally, if you look closely at couples who have low moral standards, you will discover that they are not happy. The following real-life story is a good example.

Aaron was a married man and father of two young children. He routinely had extramarital affairs. He was successful but seldom cheerful.

After years of dishonesty within his own relationship, Aaron had an affair with a married woman and mother of three. They fell madly in love and left their families to start a new life together.

When I saw Aaron several years later, he shared with me the issues in his new marriage. He and his wife were extremely unhappy. There was jealousy, suspicion, and constant fights.

I asked if he was cheating on his new wife. He confessed that he continued to seek affairs outside the relationship and even had a new mistress. In other words, there was no change in his immoral lifestyle. And he looked and sounded unhappy.

Lying and cheating are enemies of good communication. Without them, partners are able to communicate freely. Open communication enables them to understand each other, establish agreements, and work as a team to solve problems and advance in life.

The moment they start keeping secrets from each other, their communication suffers. They have to remember what they said and ensure that their new stories match the previous ones.

> ***If you tell the truth,***
> ***you don't have to remember anything.***

—Mark Twain

When partners don't tell the truth, they start to feel disconnected, as if a wall were erected between them. The bricks in the wall are the secrets they keep from each other. Those may be big secrets or small, significant or insignificant, secrets to protect themselves or to cover up for someone else. With time, the wall grows thicker and taller, until they become unable to find the connection they once had.

You may have witnessed situations such as these:

The wife sees a nice dress in a store which she falls in love with. It's over her budget but she "has to have it," so she goes ahead and buys the dress. She knows her spending would anger her husband, so when she gets home, she reports a price lower than the actual cost of the item.

The husband has stopped at a bar after work and had a drink with his friend Joe. He knows his wife doesn't like Joe because Joe is promiscuous and drinks too much. So when he gets home, he tells her that he had to work late and that traffic was bad.

There is a personal policy that I live by, which has served me well in my marriage of over three decades:

I never do anything I would not want to tell my husband about. If I have to hide it, it must be wrong. So I don't do it. It's as simple as that.

I have observed that couples who keep secrets from each other tend to pick fights. Being honest with one another is not only your moral duty, but it brings you peace of mind personally and preserves your happiness as a couple.

> ***Human happiness and moral duty are inseparably connected***
>
> —George Washington

Lack of Support

Life is no picnic. At times, it is more like a battleground. Even routine daily life can be overwhelming. From financial stress, work and career hurdles to family matters and health issues, the challenges are many. We all need help, and others need our help.

That is why we must make our relationship the safe haven where tired and wounded soldiers retreat for healing and shelter. It is where we recuperate before returning to the battlefield that is daily life.

When someone has been challenged all day, had to prove themselves to the boss, has nearly lost a deal or argued with mother over the phone, received bad news from the doctor or has just been pushing on for days without proper food or sleep, they should be able to find a safe haven in their partner. They need their partner's support.

When you return home and explode at each other, you are not being supportive. You are turning your home into a battlefield worse than the one both of you have to face in the outside world.

Being supportive requires that you observe the condition your partner is in when he or she returns from "battle" and help them recuperate from their misadventures. Do they look tired, hungry or bad-tempered? Did they have a bad day?

Support means lending an ear. Don't be quick to point out where they are wrong, even if they are. Before they recognize that the boss, mother or whoever was right after all, they might need to vent the disappointments of the day. Then, when the realization comes from them and is not something that is pushed off on them, they might benefit from it. Otherwise, they will reject any words of wisdom.

Being supportive also means encouraging them to keep going. If a business deal fell through or they failed a college exam, they don't need sympathy or to be encouraged to quit. That would be like telling a wounded soldier to give up and stay in a wheelchair for life.

Do give them care; feed them; let them rest and recover; then send them back on their way with your support and faith in their ability to win the next battle.

Being supportive of each other is a vital part of preserving your **_garden of love_**.

Don't Ruin It!

In summary, there are three main ways your relationship could get ruined. Fortunately, you have control of all of them.

First, you could neglect your garden of love. In other words, fail to preserve and nurture what you have started. That includes focusing on your careers and/or children to such an extent that you put your relationship on the back burner. You stop working to keep romance going, maintain your communication and take pleasure in one another. You put the relationship on autopilot and expect it to keep going with little effort of your own. Uncared-for gardens wither and die, and so will your relationship.

Second, you could allow exterior influences to affect that special bond you once had. Going with the flow of outside negativity lets powerful toxins in that could destroy your garden of love. So be unique, do not follow the herd and do not let negativity into your life.

Third, there could be destruction from within: some of your actions and reactions, and your partner's, are lethal garden pests. By your own behavior, you might bulldoze your garden and turn it into a desert.

So, don't ruin it! Realize that you are comrades in battle. Keep the fight on the outside, not between you. Make home the refuge where each of you finds safety, warmth, friendship, and support. Make your relationship an oasis in the desert of life, where you recharge your batteries, regain your strength and get ready to once again face the world.

When life gets tough, stay united.

Chapter 8

Sex and Your Happiness

Chapter 8 | *Sex and Your Happiness*

There is more to a relationship than sex. But if sex vanishes, or when partners' individual needs are not met, it can become a significant source of unhappiness. In some instances, it can even destroy the relationship. The following real-life story illustrates that.

Alex and Leslie had been married for some time. In recent years, their sex life had become nonexistent. He was extremely frustrated by it and considered divorce. They loved each other dearly but were at a loss for solutions. For some unknown reason, she was always fatigued and even felt depressed. She had no sex drive and her energy was extremely low.

I recommended that she see a holistic medical doctor and get her hormones and overall health checked. Sure enough, her hormones were way off. With the help of natural hormone therapy, she regained her energy. Her depression vanished, as it was caused by her low energy. After all, what fatigued person is happy? She regained her sex drive and their intimacy was rekindled. Since their relationship was otherwise good, that was the end of their trouble.

Loss of libido occurs not only in women, but in men too. It may be caused by poor health, excessive drinking, drug use (marijuana and others), prescription medication, being overweight, indulgence in video games, or pornography. The result is the same: frustration, resentment and unhappiness.

Sex is like a spice. To be nutritious, food need not be seasoned, but it certainly tastes better when it is. Similarly, sex adds flavor to a relationship. It makes partners feel desired and attractive. It creates a sense of intimacy and brings them closer emotionally. It is a part of your garden of love.

As with all other aspects of a relationship, agreement is key. For instance, if both partners enjoy an active sex life, they would be fulfilled. A couple could be equally happy if both preferred less sex. But they should see eye to eye.

As long as their needs and expectations are similar, there will be harmony.

Foreplay

Sex usually starts with foreplay. But one person's idea of foreplay may be different from the other's, as the following real-life story illustrates.

William was extremely frustrated about his sex life. It had been two months since he and his wife were intimate. Even handholding, hugs and kisses were lacking. He felt unloved.

Debbie complained that William treated her disrespectfully, which did not make her want to be intimate with him. When he came home from work, she explained, she would want to share the events of her day with him, but he wasn't interested. He would dismiss her communication and that made her feel disrespected. So at bedtime, when he wanted sex, she was feeling distant, resentful, and had no interest.

Foreplay starts with conversation. It begins in the morning, with a good-morning greeting, a hug and a kiss, and continues throughout the day by staying in touch, if at all possible, and letting each other know that you are on each other's minds, even on a busy day. It continues with good communication in the evening and up until bedtime. Then, you are ready for physical foreplay that leads to sex. Everything that led up to it might be called "emotional foreplay."

Helicopters vs. Airliners

It helps to remember that male and female bodies are different. When it comes to sex, most men are like helicopters. They go from zero to sixty in no time at all. No runway is needed.

Women, on the other hand, are more like airliners. They taxi down the runway in preparation for takeoff and, at last, start heading for the sky. Like the helicopter, they reach the clouds, but it usually takes longer.

Keeping those differences in mind could help a couple understand each other's needs and so improve their sex life.

If your relationship is bad—your communication is poor, you are often upset with each other, you are in a constant power struggle, pointing fingers and trying to get your way—then you are not setting the stage for intimate moments. Fighting and arguing are not good foreplay and neither is the absence of communication. As for makeup sex, it is a mark of an unstable, volatile, explosive relationship.

Sex is your dessert, not the main dish. It does not have what is needed to support a lifelong relationship any more than sweets could nourish your body for life.

Your friendship is your best foreplay—being close, having warm feelings toward each other, trusting and appreciating one another. That is your main dish. The dessert will follow.

How Sex Life Deteriorates

One reason your sex life may have deteriorated, if it has, is neglect of your garden of love.

Most couples make an effort to have an active sex life when they first meet. The woman appears as enthusiastic about sex as the man. The man is romantic, affectionate and complimentary. He listens to her and gives her his full attention. Both of them get the impression that their life together is going to be filled with romance and passion. When this changes later in the relationship, they are disappointed and may feel deceived. They were sold one thing and got another. The following real-life story is such an example.

When Mark and Darlene got married, they were madly in love. It was a second marriage for both and they felt blessed to have found each other. After the divorce from her first husband, Darlene stayed single for many years. She had nearly lost all hope of ever finding love again by the time she met Mark.

He seemed perfect in every way and treated her like his queen. He was attentive, generous, loving and caring. Their sex life was amazing. And he wanted to spend his life with her. She couldn't ask for anything more.

On their wedding night he changed. He became cold and uncaring. In the months to come, selfishness she had never before seen in him reared its ugly head. It manifested itself even in the bedroom, where he would satisfy himself, turn aside and fall asleep, leaving her feeling used, unloved and frustrated.

It is unfair to present a promising picture at the start of a relationship just to pull it away later. Often, sex is used in the "sales job" new couples do on each other and, although they may not mean it that way, it borders on deceit.

The daily routine of a growing family is not as sex-friendly as dating. But if your behavior promised great and loving sex when you first met, you must do your best to keep up with that first impression. In other words, tend to your garden of love as it relates to your sex life.

That does not mean putting up with unpleasant sex just to satisfy your partner. But it does mean being open about it and working together to make it a satisfying, delicious "dessert" for both of you.

Other Reasons

Neglect of the ***garden of love*** is not the only cause of sex life deterioration. Bodies change with age, illness, injuries, and self-neglect. We work them hard, use and abuse them. Women go through pregnancies, childbirth, and nights of breastfeeding. Some men experience health issues that affect their sexual performance. Drug use, excessive alcohol consumption, marijuana, and prescription drugs also do damage.

Later in life there is menopause for women and there are hormonal changes for both men and women. Those affect one's sex drive and performance, as well as one's overal quality of life. Many menopausal women are misdiagnosed with depression and prescribed drugs. What they are really going through is simply nature's Change of Life. Fortunately, modern medicine offers help in the form of natural (bioidentical) hormones and other anti-aging treatments. There are gynecologists and holistic medical doctors who focus on hormonal balancing, disease prevention and overall well-being.

Do not be offended if your partner does not respond the way he or she used to. This would be the time to exercise sensitivity, patience, and consideration while your partner works on well-being, sobriety, or both.

Sex is not a one-sided activity. It must be enjoyed by both people or it isn't worthwhile. So help each other to achieve optimum performance that brings pleasure to both of you.

The Grass Is Greener Where You Water It

Unsatisfying sex life may lead people to believe that the grass is greener on the other side. But as chef and restaurateur Wolfgang Puck said, "the grass is greener where you water it." If you tend your garden, it will flourish.

A lover or mistress may seem exciting while they hold that illicit position in your life. Marry them, and you will face the very same challenges with them that you are presently having with your significant other. Not to mention the pain and destruction your affair could bring to your family.

The truth is, cheaters are unhappy people, regardless of how much "fun" they seem to have. I have known some, and they were either bad-tempered or manifested fake joy.

They lived under the heavy burden of their dark secrets, were mean toward their partners and critical of other people in their lives.

Nothing compares to the peace of mind that comes with having nothing to hide. Being honest is so much easier than lying and cheating.

I think you will agree that there is more to sex than fulfilling a physical need or even creating babies. It is a way of expressing your love and affection and telling your partner that he or she is attractive and desirable to you. It is a way of reassuring each other of your love and should be used correctly in tending your garden of love.

Happiness is when what you think, what you say, and what you do are in harmony.

—Gandhi

Chapter 9

Settling Your Differences

Chapter 9 | *Settling Your Differences*

You will never find two identical individuals. People are unique. As a couple, most of your differences are not a matter of good or bad, just different. Your harmony and happiness do not depend on changing your partner to be like you or vice versa. Some people try, but that never works, nor is it fair or necessary. What does work is being a team and creating harmony instead of conflict.

A band or an orchestra consists of different instruments. Each has something to offer and is unique and beautiful in its own right. Making those instruments harmonize instead of clash takes work, but the result is beautiful music.

The same is true of a marriage. Working as a team—not against each other—you can create a relationship that is both harmonious and fulfilling. The following pages will show you how to settle your differences and increase your harmony.

Racehorses vs. Mules

Some people claim that opposites attract. Perhaps they do. Be that as it may, being opposites does not guarantee happiness and may cause a lot of fighting and arguing, as it did for Carl and Donna.

They were complete opposites. Carl was like a car traveling at top speed. He was active and energetic, quick to make decisions and act on them, always on the go and getting a lot done.

Donna, on the other hand, traveled in first gear. She was responsible and got things done, but at a much slower pace. She could watch TV for hours and would take all day to prepare a meal that Carl could whip up in no time at all.

The relationship was frustrating for both of them. To her, he was "impatient." To him, she was "lazy."

Carl and Donna were like a racehorse and a mule. Racehorses are faster than mules, yet mules are intelligent and have greater strength and endurance for their size. Each is beautiful and capable in its own way but, due to their differences, they must coordinate their actions if they are to pull a wagon together.

The same is true for any couple who are a racehorse-plus-mule combination. Understanding their differences would go a long way to reduce their frustrations with one another. They would know that neither of them is trying to upset the other. It is the difference between them that causes them trouble. Rather than argue or criticize each other about the way they are, they would understand that this difference requires greater coordination in pulling their wagon of life.

Having that understanding, they would work on meeting each other halfway: the racehorse would slow down while the mule would make an effort to speed up. Working that way, they would prevent fights and enjoy greater success and happiness in their relationship.

Attitude Is Everything

Another matter that could cause trouble is having different attitudes or perspectives about life.

For instance, one of you may be cheerful, positive and optimistic, while the other worries about the future or feels sad about the past. One is quick to recover from past misfortunes and face the future with renewed hope, while the other takes years to heal old wounds. Having different attitudes is hard on a relationship and could cause misunderstandings and fights, as the following real-life story illustrates.

Becky and Daniel were worlds apart. He was a happy-go-lucky fellow. She was always in low spirits. She would go to work, come home, take care of their son and the house and complain about how hard life was. Nothing cheered her up and she seldom smiled.

Daniel, on the other hand, was cheerful, motivated and worked hard to progress in his career. He loved his job and became quite successful. He also enjoyed his duties as a father. And although Becky loved their son as much as he did, she fulfilled her duties with little joy.

Daniel would share his views with her, trying hard to uplift her spirits and give her a better outlook on life, but nothing seemed to inject her with joy.

He could not understand her depressed attitude and she could not understand his cheerfulness. As a result, they argued constantly.

When one partner approaches life with hope and energy while the other is too afraid to try, when one attacks problems with determination while the other gives up without a fight, they must work harder to settle their differences.

Both must adjust. Mr. or Ms. Down must make an effort to cheer up and avoid being so negative, while Mr. or Ms. Cheerful should try to help their partner to be in better spirits.

Tolerance plays part in this. They should not criticize each other about the way they are. They should accept what is going on and try their best to understand and help one another.

They would also have to remember that factors such as hunger, tiredness and physical pain play a part in one's mood or patience and not get into discussions when they need to eat, sleep, or sober up.

Your Goals

When love is young and new, couples connect over the small things they find in common: the type of food they like, their taste in music or art, their love for movies, dance or the outdoors; the people and places they both know, or similar life experiences. And, although it is nice to have a lot in common, that is not a good enough foundation for building a lifelong relationship.

A couple is a team. Teams unite over what they are trying to accomplish together—their goals. An athletic team has the goal of winning competitions. A police squad has the goal of beating crime. A family should share the goal of helping each other do better in life and become happy, healthy and successful.

In addition to team goals, a couple should have individual goals. Just because you share your lives is no reason you should lose your individual selves. After all, you were "you" before you joined forces and became a couple. So, take into consideration your own goals and your partner's goals as well as your mutual goals.

Goals

In some relationships, one partner is domineering and has a tendency to try to control the other without taking their feelings into consideration. The one puts limitations on the other partner's goals, resulting in resentment and unhappiness.

I had a childhood friend who loved to sing. From across the street, I could hear her beautiful, powerful voice as it drowned out the loud sound of her radio.

She married young and had children. Years later she told me that her husband would not allow her to perform anywhere, not even at community events. Pursuing a career was out of the question. She was resentful and unhappy.

Had her husband been wise, he would have supported her goal. She would have been happy with the occasional local show while still being a devoted wife and mother. His dominance over her goals made for an unhappy marriage.

Another point to consider regarding goals is that while your individual goals need not be identical, they must not clash. Goals are like destinations. You journey from where you are to where you want to be—a better place or condition. You should work out how to take your individual journeys side by side rather than permit them to separate you. It is not always easy to do, but you should work to align those goals so they benefit each of you as well as your family and relationship.

The 1960s TV sitcom Green Acres features a couple who have grossly misaligned goals. New York lawyer Oliver has a dream to become a farmer and live off the land. He buys a farm and moves there with his socialite wife Lisa, who hates the countryside.

While the challenges of their misaligned goals make for good comedy, in real life they would make both people miserable.

How to Stay in Harmony

Misaligned goals could result in constant fighting and arguing. But how do you align your goals and create the harmony you have always wanted?

Your magical tool is communication. Use it well, as discussed in earlier chapters.

Tell your partner about your aspirations and let him or her tell you about theirs. Listen well. Never tell them that their goals are unattainable or unimportant, even if you cannot imagine how anyone would have such interests. These are their goals.

The only exception would be, of course, goals that are illegal, immoral, unethical, or destructive to you, your family, or anyone else. You would not support his career as a drug dealer, or hers as a stripper, for instance.

Other than that, do not worry if what you hear sounds like potential trouble.

Let's suppose he wants to live in Alaska and fish for salmon, but she can't stand the cold. Or, she aspires to be a nurse but he does not want her to be working nights.

In such cases, hear each other out. Really try to understand what your partner is saying and how they feel. You do not have to agree. You can still understand. And be sure to let them know you do.

Now, together, work out solutions. If she is so in love with the nursing idea, perhaps she could get a job at a day clinic, so night shifts do not disrupt your family life. Perhaps the two of you could visit Alaska together during the summer and he could fish for salmon for a while.

Also, remember that not all goals are created equal. Some are more important than others. Some are more productive and contributive to your family than others. Some are just nice to have but not vital. Some are way off in the future and a lot could happen between now and then. There is no need to fight over them now or debate about irrelevant details.

Calmly weigh things out and decide what could be done to help each of you pursue your dreams and find happiness. The following real-life story illustrates that.

Vicki and Ken had been married for some years and had a young daughter. Having been a stay-home mom for several years, Vicki wanted to expand her life beyond motherhood and learn a skill that would enable her to earn an income.

Ken's first reaction was to object. He was concerned about their daughter. He was willing to work harder at his job so Vicki could stay home with the girl. He wanted the peace of mind of knowing that their daughter was being cared for by the best person possible, her mother.

But Vicki's desire to work was not only about money. She wanted to have a career and an identity of her own, besides Wife and Mother.

Vicki and Ken discussed the matter at length, not arguing but hearing each other out. Ken understood why Vicki wanted to work, and she understood his concerns. They did not exchange mutual insults. They did not defend. They listened and acknowledged each other.

Finally, they came up with a solution: Vicki was going to take a bookkeeping course, most likely from home, and get licensed. She would then find a job that could be mostly done from home.

She would have a career and a way of earning income and he would have peace of mind knowing that their daughter was well cared for.

Another aspect of goals is that they may need to be updated periodically. People grow and change, and their aspirations change with them. A young couple may not have wanted children when they first met, but now they do. Where previously they may have wanted several kids, after one or two they may choose to stop and focus on their careers or hobbies. So regardless of your agreements, things could change and new agreements may need to be made.

As always, communication is your best tool. Keep it open and sincere, and permit each other to communicate anything and everything without being attacked or blamed. You will then know about any new goals or change of goals, and you could realign yourselves to each other as needed.

Balancing Your Communication

Some people are reserved and uncommunicative, while others are talkative and outgoing. Some people do not share much unless they feel it is important. Others are open about their lives and love to share every detail of their day. One partner may have been raised in a home where "children should be seen but not heard" and learned not to express his or her thoughts. The other may have had a loud home environment where, unless you learned to speak up, you would never be heard or noticed.

As a result, there may be differences in how much each of you communicates. If one of you "talks a lot," that person might overwhelm the other with communication and make him or her shut down. Their faint willingness to share their thoughts, feelings or the events of the day might be overcome by the quantity of communication directed at them. As a result, they might retreat and cease communicating.

The following real-life story illustrates that.

Kyle and Sally were on the verge of divorce. They had major communication issues. During their in-office sessions, I noticed that she would talk openly and at length about everything that bothered her. She had a lot on her mind, and she would voice it in detail, discussing one topic and moving on to the next without giving Kyle a chance to respond. She was like a fire hydrant blasting out water.

Kyle was the reserved type. During private sessions with me, he would open up. I would ask a question and sit back, interested in his response. I let him finish his sentences and allowed him to voice his views without being contradicted or criticized. He felt safe communicating with me.

Such freedom of expression did not exist in his conversations with Sally. She would interrupt to defend herself or explain her views. Because he was already a delicate and fragile communicator, that would make him pull back into his shell. He could not take the confrontation well and would cease communicating.

Who was at fault? Both took part in creating their problem. She, by being an unstoppable communication machine gun. He, by allowing himself to be overwhelmed instead of having the courage and determination to express himself and to insist that he be heard.

If you and your partner have such an issue, it is time to balance your communication.

The outgoing partner should put down their communication machine gun. Even if they have a lot to say, they must not neglect to observe their partner and ensure that the other is still listening.

Have you ever had a conversation with someone and suddenly felt like they were not with you anymore? Somewhere along the line you lost them. They stopped listening, had wandering thoughts, or imploded because they were not permitted to respond.

Or perhaps you were that person who was listening and found yourself unable to get a word in edgewise.

That's what can happen when one person overwhelms the other with communication. Instead of a conversation, you get a lecture.

To balance your communication, both of you should be able to listen as well as say your piece when it's your turn. It takes practice, but if you can do that, you will find that discussions need not lead to arguments and that you can look forward to your conversations rather than dread them.

Multitasking

People have different capabilities regarding the number of tasks they can handle at any given time. It is commonly believed that women have a greater ability to multitask than men. A woman may be cooking while rocking the baby, keeping an eye on a toddler, and answering the phone. A man might focus on the task at hand, be it checking oil in the car or repairing a lock, and not really hear what his wife is saying to him. That is not to say that one ability is better than the other—both have their advantages and disadvantages—but such differences could cause friction.

In the handling of life, multitasking is not the only difference a couple could have. There is also one's response to stress, emergencies, and unexpected events. Some people get overwhelmed by holiday events, financial pressures, or bad news, while others deal with them more calmly.

You take the kids to the playground and one of them gets hurt. One parent might get overwhelmed and be unable to think or act, while the other responds efficiently and effectively. He or she assesses the situation, determines that a visit to an urgent care clinic is in order and, in minutes, has it all arranged.

How can you best deal such differences?

With understanding and kindness.

The overwhelmed partner should do their best not to be in the way and to support the other while they handle the emergency. The person taking care of the issue should do so without using the incident to blame, belittle or invalidate their partner. You are a couple—a team. You are in it together, for better or worse. Each of you has his or her strengths and weaknesses. Support one another, and combine your strengths to make a better life for each other and for your family.

Affection

Some people express their emotions, especially those of love and affection, freely. Most young children do. Women tend to do so more than men, although that is not always the case. I have heard men complain about "not enough affection."

In a relationship where one partner desires to openly and frequently give and receive affection, while the other shows little warmth, you can expect resentment and unhappiness.

The affectionate partner feels unhappy, unheard, and unappreciated. As this resentment builds up, it threatens the relationship.

That's a shame! Because at the start of the relationship, most people show whatever affection or kindness they think will get them the "prize" that is their partner. I have known people who had pretended and played the part of the sweetest, most affectionate partner ever, only to change as soon as they have "caught their prey." That's deception.

On the other hand, some relationships begin with the affectionate partner knowing that they are getting involved with a "cold" person. They are not surprised by the lack of affection, but may still be unhappy about it.

Regardless of how it happened that those two opposites came together, they might need to change the situation in order to increase their happiness or even save the relationship.

The solution goes back to mutual tolerance and respect. If you are willing to understand each other's needs and wants and work to meet each other halfway, you will succeed. The affectionate person would feel loved and desired in the relationship, and the "colder" partner might be surprised by the advantages they gain from expressing some love.

Drive

I have known individuals who have had the perfect background for success. They came from families of means, were sent to the best schools, their college educations were paid for, or a successful family business waited for them to work in and eventually inherit. Their families were both willing and able to provide them with the best opportunities to achieve any goal they set for themselves. And what did they do? Nothing. A red carpet of opportunity had been rolled out for them and they did not bother to set foot on it. They had no drive to achieve anything nor any sense of responsibility for preserving the gifts they were given. And in many cases, they turned to drugs that completely ruined their potentially perfect lives.

On the other hand, we have all known people who came from an underprivileged or abusive background, who yet became wealthy, successful, happily married, famous, or whatever "success" meant to them. Why? They had the drive to make something of themselves, attain certain goals or carry out the mission each one had in life. They were motivated and determined.

Whatever your drive or motivation, I hope you are living it.

In relationships, if one partner is significantly more driven than the other, a couple may experience difficulties.

One of you pushes forward, wanting to get an education, build a business, have a better lifestyle or contribute to the community, while the other hopes for a calm existence. Driven people rarely have calm lives and that spills over to their family and friends.

If your partner and you do not have a similar level of drive, you must work hard to close the gap between you. Do so with the intention of helping rather than attacking each other.

The driven person could help the other rekindle some goal they may have given up long ago. And the less-driven person could help the other partner attain his or her goals, maybe not by working with them in their industry or on their projects, but by supporting them in their activities and becoming "the great woman behind the great man," or vice versa.

What a Mess!

An entirely different point of contention in relationships is how "messy" one partner is, versus the opposite: how "obsessively" clean and tidy the other may be. Many arguments revolve around such mundane issues.

When you were dating, you could not imagine fighting over leaving socks on the floor, loading up the dishwasher, or piling up mail on the kitchen counter. But here you are, living life.

While it may seem to one partner that the other is being petty, there is more to it than that. It is about feeling heard, noticed, appreciated and important.

When the wife has been asking the family to take off their shoes at the door and her requests are brushed off, she feels brushed off, unimportant, unappreciated. When the husband wants the kids to pick up their toys so he can have orderly surroundings to decompress in, after a day's work, and the wife does not back him up, he feels ignored, unimportant, and unappreciated.

It's not about the toys, the floor, the dishes or the laundry. Those are symbols, like flowers or gifts or a packed lunch. They say, "I care; your opinion matters to me; how you feel is important; I appreciate what you do; you deserve the help."

And that is why, as my clients often say, they "fight over the smallest things." Those are small indeed but as symbols, they speak volumes.

Chapter 10

Let Them Be

Chapter 10 | *Let Them Be*

Another vital aspect of human relationships has to do with letting people be who they are. In other words, respecting their views, accepting their goals and appreciating them for who they are and what they are trying to do. Have you ever wished others would treat you with such tolerance and respect?

That does not mean appreciating someone for being a serial killer. And in relationships, you would not accept abuse, infidelity, dishonesty or laziness because "that's who he is" or "that's the way she is." But you should not criticize them for being different from you. Being different does not make them wrong.

The dynamics between parents and children illustrate this well.

Many parents find it difficult to let their children be who they are. The parents' hopes and dreams for their child do not always match what the child wants for himself or herself. The parents may have dreamt of their son or daughter receiving higher education and becoming a doctor, lawyer or university professor, only to witness them turning to art, business, or blue-collar professions. A father may have hoped his son would take over the family business built with hard work and great sacrifice, only to have his hopes disappointed when the son chooses a different career path. Parents may have dreamt of one day having grandchildren who grow up next door, yet their child chooses another state, an opposite coast or a faraway land in which to build a future.

I knew a young man who was a talented pianist. He suffered his parents' disapproval for years because, they said, "Music is not a profession."

The absurd part of it was that their intolerance continued even after he had become one of the top performing pianists in his field. They were so busy disapproving of him for not being what they wanted him to be, that they could not acknowledge his many accomplishments. They simply refused to accept him for who and what he was.

In many relationships, partners find it hard to let each other be who they are. Instead, they nag and criticize, resulting in conflict and arguments. People have different tastes, opinions, goals, expectations, and points of view. After all, a relationship is a combination of two distinctly different individuals. Putting them together under the same roof in peace, love, and harmony is no small feat.

Many people criticize their partner out of the desire to help them or the situation they are in. They mean no harm. But people tend to shut down when they are met with disapproval, and so does your partner. Don't try to show him or her how wrong they are "for their own good." You may be trying to help, but your intentions will be misconstrued.

Only with tolerance and respect for the way a person is, can you make suggestions or try to contribute your knowledge and wisdom to help them. You can never do so with disapproval or fault-finding. If you make it sound like you know best, your efforts may be rejected.

It helps to remember that not everything in life is a matter of life and death, right and wrong. It may simply be a difference in taste or opinion—"my way" versus "your way"—and it is not worth a fight.

One of my clients wanted his towels folded a certain way. And once folded and put away, he insisted that the bottom towels be used before the ones on top.

If his wife accidentally used a top towel, an argument would ensue.

How important is the exact arrangement and use of towels? How deeply does it impact the family's well-being? Is it a battle worth fighting? Not likely.

There are other reasons couples have for disapproving of each other, for one criticizing the other for the way he or she is. For instance, their choice of career path or differences in ambitions or aspirations, as this real-life story illustrates.

He was a skilled blue-collar worker who made a decent living and supported his family. She came from a family of entrepreneurs and aspired to build wealth. Of course, the sky was the limit and her drive could bring them great abundance. So, while holding a job, she also put in the work toward that future prosperity.

However, she was frustrated by the fact that her husband was content with his job and not as driven as she. He would try, after a long day of work, but required her constant push. At the same time, he was a good family man, a loving husband, and a great father.

In that regard, she could not ask for more. Still, she would constantly criticize him for lacking the same entrepreneurial spirit she had.

Only when she accepted him as he was and learned to value his virtues—loyalty, consistency, steadfast work, supporting the family with his earnings and allowing her the time and means to pursue her dreams—did they find harmony. Instead of criticizing the way he was, she learned to appreciate him. Now they were able to work as a team, plan their wealth-building together, discuss the necessary steps, and agree on ways he could realistically participate in those plans.

So, let each other be. As long as your partner's actions are productive, positive and helpful, there is no need for criticism. You will always have your differences—you are two unique individuals. Learn to accept each other as you are. Tolerate the petty stuff, and respect the person that your partner is.

Let them be!

***We are** all special and different.*

—Marlone, age three

Children, Blended Families and Co-parenting

Chapter 11 | *Children, Blended Families and Co-parenting*

No relationship book is complete without touching on the subject of children. Not only because children are important, but also because a couple's different perspectives and parenting styles could greatly strain their relationship. We have had people come to us on the verge of divorce because of child-related issues. And not only in blended families, but between biological parents as well.

Parents want the best for their children and make great sacrifices to provide what they believe is needed for the raising of a happy, healthy, successful person. But life is demanding and busy with work, school, sports, financial stresses, family and social obligations, trying to keep a couple's own relationship going, and more.

Children have both physical and emotional needs. No amount of money or luxury could make up for a poor connection between parent and child.

Should You Be Your Child's Friend?

My client, a special-education teacher, said in passing, "I know you are not supposed to be your child's friend."

"I disagree," I replied. "My mother was my friend. I felt safe to communicate to her and, because of that, I was well behaved. We also shared the love of music and reading, and I became eager to learn."

Wouldn't you rather have your children confide in you than in their friends or complete strangers? Wouldn't you want them to feel comfortable to come to you for advice and know that you would not yell or lecture them but rather listen and understand? As their friend, when you gave your input, it would be well received.

This is not to say that you should not parent or even discipline your children when needed. But if you are close to them, they will understand your rules and you may find that the need for discipline is minimal.

Now remember that communication flows both ways: from you to the child and the child to you. If you always lecture or teach a child, you do not permit him or her to share their views. Children have opinions. Do not correct everything they say, if it doesn't need to be corrected. Save the corrections for vital issues.

Additionally, do not assume that they want advice. Sometimes people simply need to vent. They are not seeking solutions, only a safe space to unburden. So make it safe for your children to express their thoughts and feelings. That alone might help them gain clarity. And you may be surprised at what we, the adults, could learn from them.

The Power of Quality Time

Time is more precious than money. You could throw money and gifts at your loved ones yet deny them your time and attention. A child needs you at least as much as they need money or things. Maybe more.

Years ago, I spent a short time with a friend's son while he was taking care of some business. We walked down to a cafeteria, where the boy got himself something to eat. Then we sat at a table and talked while he had his food. There was a pond of turtles, so we looked at the turtles and chatted about them.

When he got home that afternoon he said to his mother, "Daphna is my best friend." All I had done was give him my attention and communicate with him. And we bonded.

How often do you bond with your child or children in an intimate setting and without TV, phones, video games and other distractions? Yet undivided attention and good communication are powerful tools, as the following real-life story illustrates.

A couple I was helping in my office had issues with their six-year-old son. He had been a happy boy until four years earlier, when his baby brother was born. Sharing his parents' love and attention with another child affected him deeply, so they took him to a therapist. But therapy was not working, and the boy remained gloomy.

"Your son doesn't need another stranger in his life," I told the parents. "Not me, not a therapist. He needs you!" I recommended that they start a tradition of quality time with the children: one day, Mom would spend an hour with the one boy and Dad with the other. The next day they would switch. Such time would be spent doing whatever the child pleased (barring harm to property or living things, or activities that are outside the family budget). It might be in or outdoors; might be books, art, ball games, anything.

Mom created a calendar and posted it on the refrigerator. The boy was delighted to see his name in ink and know that his private time with each parent was guaranteed. The weekly schedule permitted a day for family activities, which he did not resent, since he was fulfilled by his own dedicated time. As for the parents, they were ahead as a result of this bargain: therapy was out of town and required a full day. Now, each of them invested four hours a week and the result in terms of the children's emotional well-being was much superior.

I saw the family shortly after they had begun to follow this plan. The older boy was cheerful and outgoing. He was no longer resentful of his little brother and had become quite helpful, as big brothers should be. The parents were proud and relieved, knowing that they could make their son happy without external support. And the youngest boy smiled at me as if he knew I had something to do with all that.

As you can see, none of this took expensive gifts, fancy equipment or luxurious vacations. All that was needed was a piece of each parent—their time, attention, heart and soul which, to their son, meant a whole lot more than anything money could buy.

If you have a "problematic" child in your life, try this. You may be pleasantly surprised.

The Secret to Good Behavior

Your child's good behavior does not depend on how much you do for him or her. Many generous parents, who have provided everything imaginable to their children, wind up with ungrateful teenagers, educational failures, drug use, and other trouble. So, giving children everything, saving them from the hardship the parents may have suffered, or paving their road with opportunity does not guarantee a happy, moral, successful child.

The best way to raise a trouble-free child is to keep him or her helpful and productive. It is not mean or cruel to get a child to help or work. On the contrary: children who are contributing members of the family build a sense of self-worth, confidence, and independence. Especially if their contributions are recognized and validated.

What I have found to be successful for many of my couples is what is called a Reward Chart, Chore Chart, or Incentive Chart. You can find them online, in the bookstore, or make your own.

The chart lists chores or goals, and the child is given points or stickers for their accomplishments. They lose points for misbehavior but are given a chance to re-earn them through good actions. At the end of the week, points are added up and a reward is given: it may be anything, from ice cream to a dollar bill, or a trip to the park or the movies. I know of children whose behavior turned around miraculously through the use of this method, as the next real-life story illustrates.

Like most couples, Barbara and Bryan led busy lives. They had demanding careers and two young children, ages four and six.

At the end of a long day, they had to deal with the children's misbehavior. Everything was a struggle: dinner, bath, putting them to bed. It took both parents and lasted three hours every night. It was exhausting, and the next morning they had to get up early and do it all over again.

I recommended the reward chart and they agreed to give it a try.

The children loved the game of earning points or stickers and the rewards that came with that. Their behavior improved instantaneously. Bedtime, in all its phases—dinner, bath, bedtime story—reduced from three hours a night to one! The six-year-old, who had hated reading, even started asking for a book every time she misbehaved and wanted to re-earn lost points.

The family dynamic completely changed, and the parents had two hours for themselves every night, which was priceless for each of them individually as well as for the two of them as a couple.

Do the Kids Come Between You?

If your children come between you, it is not their fault, but yours. You have either let it happen or you outright caused it.

A couple may have different perspectives on child rearing. One of them may be strict and more disciplinary while the other may be permissive and forgiving. Naturally, each person is influenced by their own upbringing, education, what they have seen and heard, and what they have or have not experiencedduring their own childhood. Having disagreements is normal. Just don't display them in front of the kids.

Children are smart, and they try to get their way. They should, as long as what they ask for is not harmful to them, to you, to the family, to property, animals or other people. Destructive wishes should be denied. Productive or beneficial ones could be granted, even if they annoy you because you were raised differently.

But life isn't black and white. It is mostly gray. There is good and bad in every decision one makes. A couple should discuss pros and cons and act as a team. As parents, they lead the family. Leaders do not air their differences in front of their followers. They formulate the rules behind closed doors. Only then can they be a united and reassuring front before the people they lead—in this case, the children.

Children need safety and security. Parental arguments disrupt the peace and threaten the child's stability. So much so, that I have known children who would beg their parents to divorce, because life was calmer when they were apart.

Additionally, parents who display their conflicts in front of their children open themselves to manipulation and marital disaster, as the following real-life story illustrates.

When Chris and Wendy came to see me, Wendy had already moved out and was living at her mother's house, down the street from theirs. Chris stayed at home with the children.

Wendy had been feeling bullied. Chris was the type of man who believed a wife should obey her husband, and the children took his lead and started disrespecting her.

Their oldest, a nineteen-year-old girl, verbally attacked her and demanded that she move out of the house and go live with her own mother. Chris failed to defend her. Now the couple were devastated. For the first time in their twenty-year marriage, they lived apart. The life they had built together was crumbling before them, and they had no idea how to save it.

Clearly, the daughter had nothing but her own selfish interests in mind. She was either too immature to recognize the damage she was causing, or she simply did not care. Be that as it may, it was not entirely her fault—her parents had a failing grade in Parenthood.

Their situation was unacceptable, and I told them so. "If anyone should be moving out, it's your daughter," I said. "And she should be grateful that her grandmother is even willing to have her. She's an adult and no one owes her anything."

Next time Wendy and Chris came to see me, they had turned things around. Wendy had moved back home—without asking the daughter's permission. Next, they held a family meeting and advised the children that "their opinions about the parents were not needed."

From that point on, no one, not their oldest nor any other child, dared come between them.

Blended Families

The problems of blended families lie in the fact that partners think in terms of "my child" versus "your child." It is an erroneous perspective that causes serious issues between partners. When you get married, you do not marry a person—you marry a package. If your spouse's parents are ill, you now have ill relatives who need your help. Similarly, if children are a part of the package, you must consider them and their issues your own as much as your spouse's. Your feelings toward them may not be as strong, but your care should be.

Your attitudes toward all of the children should be based on logic, not emotions. When it comes to privileges, all of them should be rewarded based on their behavior and contribution to the family. If your child misbehaves while your spouse's child is helpful and appreciative, the good behavior should be rewarded. And when it is, that does not mean that your spouse is biased in favor of their child or does not care about yours.

The issue of the *power struggle* comes into play. The wife complains about his leniency toward "his" child while he is strict with "hers." The husband claims that she babies "her" child and ignores "his." Finger-pointing takes place and matters get more passionate than ever, with each parent acting as though they are defending their child's life.

The two of you have joined your lives with the hope of living happily ever after. But being happy as a couple must include your individual happiness. If one of you is unhappy because his or her child is doing poorly, your relationship will suffer. So act as though your partner's child-related issues are your own. Because, through him or her, they are.

Co-parenting

Not all couples are fortunate enough to raise their children under one roof. A previously-failed marriage or relationship may have left one or both of you with the challenge of sharing parental responsibilities with an ex.

Reaching agreement can be hard for any couple. Agreeing with an ex may be even harder. Clearly, you have had your disagreements, or you might still be together. Yet now, for the sake of the children, you are stuck having your ex in your life.

The watchword is: Do what is best for the children. Set your differences aside and fulfill your obligations as parents.

You need to create a safe and calm atmosphere. Do not argue or fight in front of the children. Never bad-mouth your ex to a child, no matter how you feel about him or her. Keep your opinions to yourself or share them with an adult if you must, but only when the children are not within earshot.

Do not use the kids to hurt your ex—for example, by denying access to children. Doing so hurts the child.

And never allow the children to stir up trouble between you.

Abandon your *power struggle*. You must set aside any bitter feelings you may have toward each other and act as a team. Unite in the common purpose of helping your children and minimize the hardship caused by your split-up.

The Curse Called "Devices"

It used to be that only TV threatened to turn us into zombies. In today's electronic age, screens are in front of us constantly. Phones, watches, computers, tablets; even children's toys have moving, talking, singing pictures.

Moving images seem to have a hypnotizing effect on the viewer. Have you ever had a hard time turning off the TV when you knew better than to stay up late or neglect important work or study?

Dependency on screens starts at a young age. Parents are proud to provide their children with their private bedrooms, each equipped with its own television set. Why does a young child, who is natively creative, need constant entertainment? All that does is destroy his or her creativity.

Screens are habit forming. Let's face it. There is a lot of good stuff out there, and it is tempting. It is entertaining and requires no effort. Like fast food, it is an easy, instant solution with long-term consequences.

I have met young couples with serious marital issues because the husband spent hours playing video games each week or the wife was on YouTube or scrolling through social media for hours at a time. Their communication and intimacy suffered, and they were growing apart.

When it comes to child-rearing, TV, phones, tablets and electronic games are cheap babysitters. They are right there, no scheduling needed, and the child stops bothering you. You pay the price later, when you realize that you have raised a teenager who is locked up in their room playing games, talking to their friends, or getting an "education" from YouTube. They come out to eat but have no interest in helping around the house, communicating with you or spending time with the family.

When I see parents trying to keep an infant entertained by holding a phone screen in front of their face, I see an addiction in the making and the death of creativity.

You should want to preserve the creativity with which your child was born. Their success and happiness depend on it. Creative people have the ability to take initiative, solve problems and come up with new ideas. Such ability is required for their success in any job, career or business as well as in the day-to-day activities of homemaking and raising their future family.

By introducing children to TV and other devices at an early age, you condition them to continuously absorb information.

They are bombarded by it, leaving little room for their own input or creativity.

Devices produce another side effect, as the following real–life story illustrates.

One of my couples used to bring their sons along whenever they came for their sessions. They were nice boys, ages five and seven. When children come to my office, I always ask, "Do you like crayons?" I have never met a child who doesn't.

So, I would seat the boys in the lobby with crayons and sketch pads and they would keep themselves entertained. Every now and then one of them would come in to share his latest "masterpiece." We would admire it, and he would go back to his work. When the session was over, I would offer to tear the boys' art out of the sketch pads, and they would carry them home, hopping happily out the door. They were always more cheerful leaving than when they came in.

One evening when the family walked in, the boys carried their parents' phones in their hands. They were not interested in crayons and wanted to keep watching the screens. An hour later, when the session was over, the parents and I came out to find two cranky boys. They were whiny and tired; and their usual cheerful energy was nonexistent.

That was a live demonstration of Crayons vs. Devices. Crayons win!

If we want to raise successful children, we have to keep them active, creative and motivated throughout their childhood. Yes, it is a lot more work for the parents, and we live in an age of laziness.

We also must set a good example for them by not spending our own lives absorbing instead of doing. Watching screens is a waste of precious time that we could use to bond with our spouse or children, get a degree, start a side business, or otherwise advance our lives.

The Truth about ADHD

Going down a slope on a morning hike, my husband and I ran into a family on their way up the hill. Leading the pack was a young boy, six or seven years old. He was running ahead of everyone. "Don't we all wish we had this kind of energy?" my husband joked, and the adults in the group smiled and agreed.

Children have excess energy, which most adults find difficult to tolerate. Kittens do too. And even mama cat gets annoyed every now and then. Kittens grow out of it, and so do children. That is the way of nature.

But before they have a chance to grow up naturally, many children are diagnosed with Attention Deficit Disorder (ADD) or Attention Deficit Hyperactivity Disorder (ADHD) and prescribed drugs.

According to Dr. Mary Ann Block, author of *No More ADHD*, "There is no test to prove someone has [ADHD]." "The National Institute of Health has stated that there is no objective test for ADHD," she continues. "The teachers and parents fill out a checklist of symptoms. No lab is drawn, no physical exam is usually performed. Most doctors just look at the checklist and give the diagnosis and a prescription for a drug. Nowhere else in medicine does this occur."

The diagnostic checklist **Dr. Block** talks about includes: "Often fails to give close attention…" "Often does not listen…" "Often fidgets or taps hands…" "Often talks excessively…" "Is often on the go…" Only six symptoms are required to diagnose a child with ADHD.

I don't know about what you've seen, but all young children I have ever known behaved that way: my classmates, my brother, cousins I grew up with. When my stepson was very young, he was constantly on the go. He would walk on his hands in front of us practicing his gymnastics whenever we went out. He grew up to be a fine young man. And that excess energy? It was a sign of what was to come: a dynamic adult who has what it takes to handle life and become a success.

Another disturbing fact about ADHD is that it was actually voted into existence.

According to *The History of ADHD* in *www.healthline.com*, "It wasn't until the 1960s that the American Psychiatric Association formally recognized it as a mental disorder." And in 1987 members of the American Psychiatric Association voted it into existence by a show of hands. Not very scientific.

Many years ago, a mother sought my advice regarding her eight-year-old son. Bobby was hyperactive, determined his school, and needed medication. Although the mother was employed by a prominent medical group, she hesitated to drug her son and sought a second opinion outside the medical circles.

I invited them to come over. I served juice and snacks and chatted with the boy. I showed him around my office. He was interested in everything and eager to communicate. I thought he was extremely bright; but I could see the challenge his teacher must face dealing with him in the midst of thirty other children. He was dynamic and had a tremendous potential, over and above the average child. Because I had found that the brighter children are the ones to get diagnosed with ADHD, I predicted that he would grow up to be a successful adult.

When Bobby was out of earshot, I said to the mom, "Your son 'suffers' from childhood. Let him grow up." I recommended that she transfer him to a school that would cater to his needs rather than push medication on him.

She did. It so happened that a good friend of mine had her son in the same school, and the boys became best friends. For years to come, I would get updates from my friend about Bobby. He matured just fine, graduated from high school and moved on to have a successful life.

Bobby was a child who would have been medicated and ruined in an effort to make him fit in. ADHD drugs are stimulants, similar to cocaine and methamphetamines. They are addictive and can have serious side effects, including aggression, depression, seizures, stunted growth, violent behavior, and suicidal thoughts, to name a few. Yes, the child becomes "focused" and easier to manage, but there is too high a price to pay.

Over the long course of my involvement in the field of drug rehabilitation and prevention, I have come across many meth and cocaine addicts who had been diagnosed with ADHD and prescribed medication at a young age. And that was the start of their addiction.

ADHD diagnosis has been expanded to adults. I have met lawyers, nurses, doctors and members of other professions who wear this mental health label like a badge of honor. These are accomplished individuals who are far from being "mentally ill."

One attorney told me that his Adderall addiction had started in law school, where students would use the drug to stay up all night studying for exams. They had a prescription for the drug but, other than that, they were not different from meth and cocaine addicts on a drug binge.

So, before you agree to label yourself or your child with a mental disorder (illness) and have such psychiatric diagnosis entered on the medical records, do your research. Dr. Block's book is a good start and so is *www.cchrint.org*. Both provide vital yet little-known insights.

Autism Spectrum Disorder

I would be remiss in my duty if I did not quote Dr. Mary Ann Block on the subject of autism. Again, a child's problem becomes the couple's burden and could greatly affect their relationship.

Growing up I knew only one child who had developmental disabilities. In those days, such children were referred to as "retarded." However, the neighborhood kids were accepting of her and welcomed her participation in games.

Nowadays, developmental disabilities are common, with some families having more than one affected child. The current label is Autism Spectrum Disorder (ASD).

What is the cause of this modern-day epidemic? On her website, Dr. Mary Ann Block declares, "While many say they do not know what causes ASD, there are over 100 studies that tie vaccine use to ASD. Many parents will tell you how their child was perfectly normal, and speaking, and after a set of vaccines, all that went away."

For more information, visit Dr. Mary Ann Block's site at *www.BlockCenter.com*.

Chapter 12

Start Communicating!

Chapter 12 | *Start Communicating!*

You may not believe me when I say that some couples do not communicate at all. "We don't talk," I often hear. They did, when they first met. Some even thought they were marrying their best friend. But over the years, their communication became transactional rather than emotional. Now they talk about day-to-day matters of picking up the kids, the bills or what's for dinner. They no longer share their inner worlds, their thoughts and feelings with each other. As a result, they feel disconnected.

If you want to reconnect, start communicating. Talk, listen, share.

I know that it is easier said than done. You have probably tried, more than once. And you have encountered the same obstacles my clients have: "everything turns into an argument." So let me share with you some additional strategies that couples find helpful in improving their communication.

But before I do, I must stress that the following tools will not work, as long as you violate those covered in earlier chapters. For instance, if you do not choose the right time to talk; if you point fingers at each other and engage in a power struggle; if you jump topics; if you assume; if you utilize the wrong tone; if you cheat or lie; then all the strategies I provide you will be useless. Skills build one upon the other. When you learn something new, it is meant to add to your previous knowledge, not replace it. So, keep using what you have learned so far, and add the following.

They Don't Listen

One complaint I hear often is, "I try to talk to him (or her) but he doesn't listen." Then I turn to the partner for his or her perspective. After all, every coin has two sides. He usually says, "She always talks to me when I'm in the middle of something." He may be watching a game or a show, answering a text or doing a repair. In other words, he is preoccupied and she does not have his undivided attention.

Now the person initiating the communication feels ignored and unimportant and becomes resentful.

The solution is this: before you start talking to your partner, make sure they are ready to listen. Walk over and say, "Can I talk to you?" or "Let me know when you're available, I want to tell you something."

The same is true of children. If you shoot questions or orders at a child while he or she is engaged in a game, you will be ignored. Before the child is able to hear you, the child must pause what they are doing.

In other words, whomever you talk to needs to be mentally available to hear you out: not preoccupied with something else, not exhausted to the point of falling asleep in the middle of the conversation, or so hungry that all they can think about is their growling stomach.

A good strategy is to keep a list of topics you wish to discuss with your spouse or partner: those deeper issues or long-term plans; new suggestions you may have; or some incident or behavior that offended you and which you want addressed. Instead of bringing those up in the heat of the moment, put them down on your list. Then let him or her know that you wish to talk, find the right time, and have a discussion.

Eye Contact

I was working with a couple that was having severe communication issues. I noticed that they never looked at one another while talking. "Do you look at each other when you talk?" I inquired. They did not. The wife admitted that making eye contact was difficult for her. She even had a hard time looking me in the eye. And the husband seemed to direct his communication to midair, not to anyone in particular.

Eye contact is necessary for effective communication. There is no need to stare at a person while talking to him or her, but you must observe them. How are they receiving your communication? Are they listening? Do they need to respond? Because you could lose them in conversation.

Has it ever happened that you were going along sharing something when the person you were talking to mentally "left?" Their body was still there, but you could see in their eyes that they were no longer listening. Perhaps they remembered some emergency; or there was something they wanted to say in response; or they misunderstood something you said or objected to it. How would you know if you were not looking at them?

The same is true for the listener. He or she should make eye contact with the person who is talking to them.

One of my clients complained that her husband would constantly interrupt her communication. It was extremely frustrating for her, yet he did not know he was doing so. Every time he interrupted, he believed she was actually done talking. Why? He was not making eye contact. Had he been looking at her, he would have noticed that she would pause to collect her thoughts and formulate her message. She was not done talking.

So, make eye contact and observe the person you are talking or listening to. Doing so could greatly improve your communication.

Copy That

To copy, in military or radio communication, means *to acknowledge receipt of a message* (Merriam-Webster Dictionary). When someone hears something over a walkie-talkie and replies "Copy," or "Copy that," he informs the speaker that their communication has been heard and understood.

"What does this have to do with marital communication?" you ask. The following real-life story illustrates that.

Julie and Keith were a good couple. They were professionals who were devoted to each other and dedicated to their family and their four children. Yet, their communication was strained.

Julie felt that Keith never listened to her, although he really tried. He was interested in what she had to say about the children, her work, her feelings and thoughts. But somehow, she always felt unheard or misunderstood.

An intelligent and dynamic man, Keith wanted to respond to Julie's communication with advice and solutions and wondered why they would wind up arguing. He found out during our session that she did not seek advice. Most of the time, all she wished to do was share what was on her mind and be heard.

That's where "copy that" came in. The moment Keith realized that his wife did not always need or want his input, he started lending an ear and letting her know that she had been heard and understood.

I am sure there have been times when you wanted to share some occurrence or thought with someone. You were not looking for a life lesson; you did not want to be told whether you were right or wrong; you just wanted to get something off your chest and feel heard and understood. Instead, the person you were talking to was trying to be helpful in a way that you did not need or want.

Similarly, there are times when your spouse or partner wants to share, and all they want is an ear. Lend it to them, then simply let them know that you "copy that."

<hr>

Smart Relationship Analysis™ and Couples' Quiz

<hr>

Smart Relationship Analysis | *Couples' Quiz*

How good is your relationship? Is it deteriorating or improving? Is it falling apart or is it solid? Is it a "fixer-upper" or just in need of touch-ups?

Let me introduce the **Smart Relationship Analysis** and **Couples' Quiz** used to identify key issues that make or break relationships. They are based on decades of experience helping people from all walks of life save their relationships with practical, common-sense strategies. Now you can use them to get the most out of the tools in this book.

You will get a score that indicates the health of your relationship. That score provides much more than an analysis because it also shows a path to bettering your relationship, to communicating instead of fighting and to making your **garden of love** flourish.

However, the one ingredient only you can provide is determination. If both of you are committed to working toward healing, improving, repairing and rebuilding your relationship, and if you follow the advice and tools in this book, you *can* raise your score and get the relationship into excellent shape.

There have even been instances where one partner, all on his or her own, was able to raise the couple's relationship score using the tools in this book. But that depends on the nature and severity of the issues and one's persistence in application. So, answer the following questions honestly, and let's see where this quiz takes you.

Instructions

1. Answer the quiz. There are two sets of questions, one for men and one for women.

2. Add the number of *Yes* answers, *No* answers, and *Sometimes* answers and enter them in the chart at the end of the quiz. Then follow the instructions to get your score and grade.

3. This quiz is provided three times in the following pages of this book. After taking it the first time, look over the questions and find a *No* answer that you would like to address.

    Now find the chapter that contains the tools needed to deal with that issue. For example, if you answered *No* to question number twelve: *Do you work as a team?* go back and review Chapter 3, **The Power Struggle**. Then start using those tools in your daily life.

    Do the same to address other issues, as indicated by your *No* answers.

4. A month later, retake the quiz. Has your score improved? Is there more room for improvement? If so, repeat step 3 and address any *No* answers by applying the relevant tools. Do the same for your *Sometimes* answers.

5. Repeat step 4 a third time or as many times
    as needed until you are satisfied with the condition
    of your relationship.

Do not forget that, like the rest of life, a relationship is a work in progress. Never neglect it or put it on autopilot, as it *will* deteriorate.

Couples' Quiz #1
for Women

Couples' Quiz #1 | *For Women*

1) At the end of your day, do you look forward to seeing him again?
   ☐Yes ☐No ☐Sometimes

2) Are you respectful toward him?
   ☐Yes ☐No ☐Sometimes

3) Do you feel respected by him?
   ☐Yes ☐No ☐Sometimes

4) Are you able to have a disagreement without cussing or yelling at each other?
   ☐Yes ☐No ☐Sometimes

5) Are you happy with him?
   ☐Yes ☐No ☐Sometimes

6) Are you able to have a conversation without ending up in an argument?
   ☐Yes ☐No ☐Sometimes

7) Do you spend alone time as a couple?
   ☐Yes ☐No ☐Sometimes

8) Do you do special things to make him feel
   loved or appreciated?
   ☐Yes ☐No ☐Sometimes

9) Before starting a conversation, do you take into
   consideration whether or not he is tired, hungry,
   stressed, unwell, or under the influence?
   ☐Yes ☐No ☐Sometimes

10) Before reacting, do you ask yourself whether
    or not you are tired, hungry, stressed, unwell,
    PMSing, or under the influence?
    ☐Yes ☐No ☐Sometimes

11) Are you able to work on your issues without
    competing over who is better or smarter,
    who is right or wrong?
    ☐Yes ☐No ☐Sometimes

12) Do you work as a team?
    ☐Yes ☐No ☐Sometimes

13) In conversation, are you able to stay on point
    without bouncing from topic to topic?
    ☐Yes ☐No ☐Sometimes

14) Are you able to have conversations without misunderstandings?

☐Yes ☐No ☐Sometimes

15) Does he use a good tone when speaking with you?

☐Yes ☐No ☐Sometimes

16) Do you think you use a good tone when speaking with him?

☐Yes ☐No ☐Sometimes

17) During conversations, do you feel understood?

☐Yes ☐No ☐Sometimes

18) Do you feel loved?

☐Yes ☐No ☐Sometimes

19) Does he make you feel special?

☐Yes ☐No ☐Sometimes

20) Do you think he feels loved by you?

☐Yes ☐No ☐Sometimes

21) Do you feel in love and as close as you used to be?

☐Yes ☐No ☐Sometimes

22) Do you stay away from TV, phone, and social media in order to spend time together?
☐Yes ☐No ☐Sometimes

23) Are you able to see the good in him without focusing on the negative?
☐Yes ☐No ☐Sometimes

24) Is he able to see the good in you without focusing on the negative?
☐Yes ☐No ☐Sometimes

25) Do you trust him?
☐Yes ☐No ☐Sometimes

26) Does he trust you?
☐Yes ☐No ☐Sometimes

27) Do you feel like you are getting the support you need from him?
☐Yes ☐No ☐Sometimes

28) Are you supportive of him?
☐Yes ☐No ☐Sometimes

29) Are you happy with your sex life?

☐Yes ☐No ☐Sometimes

30) Do you think he is happy with your sex life?

☐Yes ☐No ☐Sometimes

31) Do you feel that you are able to achieve
your goals within the relationship?

☐Yes ☐No ☐Sometimes

32) Do you feel that he is able to achieve
his goals within the relationship?

☐Yes ☐No ☐Sometimes

33) Do you work together on common goals?

☐Yes ☐No ☐Sometimes

34) Do you think he is truthful?

☐Yes ☐No ☐Sometimes

35) Does he think that you are truthful?

☐Yes ☐No ☐Sometimes

36) Do you feel that you are able to be
yourself in the relationship?

☐Yes ☐No ☐Sometimes

37) **Do you feel** like you permit him to be himself in the relationship?
☐Yes ☐No ☐Sometimes

38) **Do you feel heard?**
☐Yes ☐No ☐Sometimes

39) **Do you think** he feels heard?
☐Yes ☐No ☐Sometimes

40) **Do you make** eye contact while talking?
☐Yes ☐No ☐Sometimes

41) **Do you share** your feelings with him?
☐Yes ☐No ☐Sometimes

42) **Does he share** his feelings with you?
☐Yes ☐No ☐Sometimes

43) **As a couple,** do you have good communication?
☐Yes ☐No ☐Sometimes

44) **Do you feel** appreciated by him?
☐Yes ☐No ☐Sometimes

45) Do you think he feels appreciated by you?
☐Yes ☐No ☐Sometimes

46) Do you admire him for his accomplishments?
☐Yes ☐No ☐Sometimes

47) Does he admire your accomplishments?
☐Yes ☐No ☐Sometimes

48) Do you express affection toward each other?
☐Yes ☐No ☐Sometimes

49) Do you hold hands in public?
☐Yes ☐No ☐Sometimes

50) Do you help each other?
☐Yes ☐No ☐Sometimes

Smart Relationship Analysis
Quiz #1 Score

Add up how many *Yes, No* and *Sometimes* answers you got.
Multiply each by the number of points indicated.
(*No* answers receive zero points.)

of *Yes* answers_________________ x 2 points = ____________

of *No* answers_________________ x 0 points = _____0_____

of *Sometimes* answers__________ x 1 point   =____________

Total: ____________

YOUR SCORE	YOUR GRADE
90-10	Excellent
80-89	Good
50-79	Coping
30-49	At Risk
0-29	Failing

Couples' Quiz #1 for Men

Couples' Quiz #1 | *For Men*

1) At the end of your day, do you look forward to seeing her again?

   ☐Yes ☐No ☐Sometimes

2) Are you respectful toward her?

   ☐Yes ☐No ☐Sometimes

3) Do you feel respected by her?

   ☐Yes ☐No ☐Sometimes

4) Are you able to have a disagreement without cussing or yelling at each other?

   ☐Yes ☐No ☐Sometimes

5) Are you happy with her?

   ☐Yes ☐No ☐Sometimes

6) Are you able to have a conversation without ending up in an argument?

   ☐Yes ☐No ☐Sometimes

7) Do you spend alone time as a couple?
☐Yes ☐No ☐Sometimes

8) Do you do special things to make her feel
loved or appreciated?
☐Yes ☐No ☐Sometimes

9) Before starting a conversation, do you take into
consideration whether or not she is tired, hungry,
stressed, unwell, PMSing, or under the influence?
☐Yes ☐No ☐Sometimes

10) Before reacting, do you ask yourself whether
or not you are tired, hungry, stressed, unwell,
or under the influence?
☐Yes ☐No ☐Sometimes

11) Are you able to work on your issues without
competing over who is better or smarter,
who is right or wrong?
☐Yes ☐No ☐Sometimes

12) Do you work as a team?
☐Yes ☐No ☐Sometimes

13) In conversation, are you able to stay on point
without bouncing from topic to topic?
☐Yes ☐No ☐Sometimes

14) Are you able to have conversations
without misunderstandings?
☐Yes ☐No ☐Sometimes

15) Does she use a good tone when speaking with you?
☐Yes ☐No ☐Sometimes

16) Do you think you use a good tone when
speaking with her?
☐Yes ☐No ☐Sometimes

17) During conversations, do you feel understood?
☐Yes ☐No ☐Sometimes

18) Do you feel loved?
☐Yes ☐No ☐Sometimes

19) Does she make you feel special?
☐Yes ☐No ☐Sometimes

20) Do you think she feels loved by you?
☐Yes ☐No ☐Sometimes

21) Do you feel in love and as close as you used to be?
☐Yes ☐No ☐Sometimes

22) Do you stay away from TV, phone, and social media in order to spend time together?

☐Yes ☐No ☐Sometimes

23) Are you able to see the good in her without focusing on the negative?

☐Yes ☐No ☐Sometimes

24) Is she able to see the good in you without focusing on the negative?

☐Yes ☐No ☐Sometimes

25) Do you trust her?

☐Yes ☐No ☐Sometimes

26) Does she trust you?

☐Yes ☐No ☐Sometimes

27) Do you feel like you are getting the support you need from her?

☐Yes ☐No ☐Sometimes

28) Are you supportive of her?

☐Yes ☐No ☐Sometimes

29) Are you happy with your sex life?
☐Yes ☐No ☐Sometimes

30) Do you think she is happy with your sex life?
☐Yes ☐No ☐Sometimes

31) Do you feel that you are able to achieve your goals within the relationship?
☐Yes ☐No ☐Sometimes

32) Do you feel that she is able to achieve her goals within the relationship?
☐Yes ☐No ☐Sometimes

33) Do you work together on common goals?
☐Yes ☐No ☐Sometimes

34) Do you think she is truthful?
☐Yes ☐No ☐Sometimes

35) Does she think that you are truthful?
☐Yes ☐No ☐Sometimes

36) Do you feel that you are able to be yourself in the relationship?
☐Yes ☐No ☐Sometimes

37) Do you feel like you permit her to be herself in the relationship?

☐Yes ☐No ☐Sometimes

38) Do you feel heard?

☐Yes ☐No ☐Sometimes

39) Do you think she feels heard?

☐Yes ☐No ☐Sometimes

40) Do you make eye contact while talking?

☐Yes ☐No ☐Sometimes

41) Do you share your feelings with her?

☐Yes ☐No ☐Sometimes

42) Does she share her feelings with you?

☐Yes ☐No ☐Sometimes

43) As a couple, do you have good communication?

☐Yes ☐No ☐Sometimes

44) Do you feel appreciated by her?

☐Yes ☐No ☐Sometimes

45) Do you think she feels appreciated by you?
☐Yes ☐No ☐Sometimes

46) Do you admire her for her accomplishments?
☐Yes ☐No ☐Sometimes

47) Does she admire your accomplishments?
☐Yes ☐No ☐Sometimes

48) Do you express affection toward each other?
☐Yes ☐No ☐Sometimes

49) Do you hold hands in public?
☐Yes ☐No ☐Sometimes

50) Do you help each other?
☐Yes ☐No ☐Sometimes

Smart Relationship Analysis
| *Quiz #1 Score*

Add up how many *Yes*, *No* and *Sometimes* answers you got.
Multiply each by the number of points indicated.
(*No* answers receive zero points.)

\# of *Yes* answers_______________ x 2 points = ______________

\# of *No* answers_______________ x 0 points = ______0______

\# of *Sometimes* answers_________ x 1 point   =______________

Total: ______________

YOUR SCORE	YOUR GRADE
90-10	Excellent
80-89	Good
50-79	Coping
30-49	At Risk
0-29	Failing

Couples' Quiz #2
for Women

Couples' Quiz #2 | *For Women*

1) At the end of your day, do you look forward
to seeing him again?

   ☐Yes ☐No ☐Sometimes

2) Are you respectful toward him?

   ☐Yes ☐No ☐Sometimes

3) Do you feel respected by him?

   ☐Yes ☐No ☐Sometimes

4) Are you able to have a disagreement without
cussing or yelling at each other?

   ☐Yes ☐No ☐Sometimes

5) Are you happy with him?

   ☐Yes ☐No ☐Sometimes

6) Are you able to have a conversation without
ending up in an argument?

   ☐Yes ☐No ☐Sometimes

7) Do you spend alone time as a couple?
□Yes □No □Sometimes

8) Do you do special things to make him feel loved or appreciated?
□Yes □No □Sometimes

9) Before starting a conversation, do you take into consideration whether or not he is tired, hungry, stressed, unwell, or under the influence?
□Yes □No □Sometimes

10) Before reacting, do you ask yourself whether or not you are tired, hungry, stressed, unwell, PMSing, or under the influence?
□Yes □No □Sometimes

11) Are you able to work on your issues without competing over who is better or smarter, who is right or wrong?
□Yes □No □Sometimes

12) Do you work as a team?
□Yes □No □Sometimes

13) In conversation, are you able to stay on point without bouncing from topic to topic?
□Yes □No □Sometimes

14) Are you able to have conversations without misunderstandings?

☐Yes ☐No ☐Sometimes

15) Does he use a good tone when speaking with you?

☐Yes ☐No ☐Sometimes

16) Do you think you use a good tone when speaking with him?

☐Yes ☐No ☐Sometimes

17) During conversations, do you feel understood?

☐Yes ☐No ☐Sometimes

18) Do you feel loved?

☐Yes ☐No ☐Sometimes

19) Does he make you feel special?

☐Yes ☐No ☐Sometimes

20) Do you think he feels loved by you?

☐Yes ☐No ☐Sometimes

21) Do you feel in love and as close as you used to be?

☐Yes ☐No ☐Sometimes

22) Do you stay away from TV, phone, and social media in order to spend time together?

☐Yes ☐No ☐Sometimes

23) Are you able to see the good in him without focusing on the negative?

☐Yes ☐No ☐Sometimes

24) Is he able to see the good in you without focusing on the negative?

☐Yes ☐No ☐Sometimes

25) Do you trust him?

☐Yes ☐No ☐Sometimes

26) Does he trust you?

☐Yes ☐No ☐Sometimes

27) Do you feel like you are getting the support you need from him?

☐Yes ☐No ☐Sometimes

28) Are you supportive of him?

☐Yes ☐No ☐Sometimes

29) Are you happy with your sex life?
☐Yes ☐No ☐Sometimes

30) Do you think he is happy with your sex life?
☐Yes ☐No ☐Sometimes

31) Do you feel that you are able to achieve
your goals within the relationship?
☐Yes ☐No ☐Sometimes

32) Do you feel that he is able to achieve
his goals within the relationship?
☐Yes ☐No ☐Sometimes

33) Do you work together on common goals?
☐Yes ☐No ☐Sometimes

34) Do you think he is truthful?
☐Yes ☐No ☐Sometimes

35) Does he think that you are truthful?
☐Yes ☐No ☐Sometimes

36) Do you feel that you are able to be
yourself in the relationship?
☐Yes ☐No ☐Sometimes

37) Do you feel like you permit him to be himself in the relationship?

☐Yes ☐No ☐Sometimes

38) Do you feel heard?

☐Yes ☐No ☐Sometimes

39) Do you think he feels heard?

☐Yes ☐No ☐Sometimes

40) Do you make eye contact while talking?

☐Yes ☐No ☐Sometimes

41) Do you share your feelings with him?

☐Yes ☐No ☐Sometimes

42) Does he share his feelings with you?

☐Yes ☐No ☐Sometimes

43) As a couple, do you have good communication?

☐Yes ☐No ☐Sometimes

44) Do you feel appreciated by him?

☐Yes ☐No ☐Sometimes

45) Do you think he feels appreciated by you?
☐Yes ☐No ☐Sometimes

46) Do you admire him for his accomplishments?
☐Yes ☐No ☐Sometimes

47) Does he admire your accomplishments?
☐Yes ☐No ☐Sometimes

48) Do you express affection toward each other?
☐Yes ☐No ☐Sometimes

49) Do you hold hands in public?
☐Yes ☐No ☐Sometimes

50) Do you help each other?
☐Yes ☐No ☐Sometimes

Smart Relationship Analysis
| *Quiz #2 Score*

Add up how many *Yes*, *No* and *Sometimes* answers you got.
Multiply each by the number of points indicated.
(*No* answers receive zero points.)

\# of *Yes* answers_______________ x 2 points = ___________

\# of *No* answers_______________ x 0 points = _____0_____

\# of *Sometimes* answers_________ x 1 point =___________

Total: ___________

YOUR SCORE	YOUR GRADE
90-10	Excellent
80-89	Good
50-79	Coping
30-49	At Risk
0-29	Failing

Couples' Quiz #2 for Men

Couples' Quiz #2 | *For Men*

1) At the end of your day, do you look forward to seeing her again?

    ☐Yes ☐No ☐Sometimes

2) Are you respectful toward her?

    ☐Yes ☐No ☐Sometimes

3) Do you feel respected by her?

    ☐Yes ☐No ☐Sometimes

4) Are you able to have a disagreement without cussing or yelling at each other?

    ☐Yes ☐No ☐Sometimes

5) Are you happy with her?

    ☐Yes ☐No ☐Sometimes

6) Are you able to have a conversation without ending up in an argument?

    ☐Yes ☐No ☐Sometimes

7) Do you spend alone time as a couple?
☐Yes ☐No ☐Sometimes

8) Do you do special things to make her feel loved or appreciated?
☐Yes ☐No ☐Sometimes

9) Before starting a conversation, do you take into consideration whether or not she is tired, hungry, stressed, unwell, PMSing, or under the influence?
☐Yes ☐No ☐Sometimes

10) Before reacting, do you ask yourself whether or not you are tired, hungry, stressed, unwell, or under the influence?
☐Yes ☐No ☐Sometimes

11) Are you able to work on your issues without competing over who is better or smarter, who is right or wrong?
☐Yes ☐No ☐Sometimes

12) Do you work as a team?
☐Yes ☐No ☐Sometimes

13) In conversation, are you able to stay on point without bouncing from topic to topic?
☐Yes ☐No ☐Sometimes

14) Are you able to have conversations without misunderstandings?

☐Yes ☐No ☐Sometimes

15) Does she use a good tone when speaking with you?

☐Yes ☐No ☐Sometimes

16) Do you think you use a good tone when speaking with her?

☐Yes ☐No ☐Sometimes

17) During conversations, do you feel understood?

☐Yes ☐No ☐Sometimes

18) Do you feel loved?

☐Yes ☐No ☐Sometimes

19) Does she make you feel special?

☐Yes ☐No ☐Sometimes

20) Do you think she feels loved by you?

☐Yes ☐No ☐Sometimes

21) Do you feel in love and as close as you used to be?

☐Yes ☐No ☐Sometimes

22) Do you stay away from TV, phone, and social media in order to spend time together?

☐Yes ☐No ☐Sometimes

23) Are you able to see the good in her without focusing on the negative?

☐Yes ☐No ☐Sometimes

24) Is she able to see the good in you without focusing on the negative?

☐Yes ☐No ☐Sometimes

25) Do you trust her?

☐Yes ☐No ☐Sometimes

26) Does she trust you?

☐Yes ☐No ☐Sometimes

27) Do you feel like you are getting the support you need from her?

☐Yes ☐No ☐Sometimes

28) Are you supportive of her?

☐Yes ☐No ☐Sometimes

29) Are you happy with your sex life?

☐Yes   ☐No   ☐Sometimes

30) Do you think she is happy with your sex life?

☐Yes   ☐No   ☐Sometimes

31) Do you feel that you are able to achieve
your goals within the relationship?

☐Yes   ☐No   ☐Sometimes

32) Do you feel that she is able to achieve
her goals within the relationship?

☐Yes   ☐No   ☐Sometimes

33) Do you work together on common goals?

☐Yes   ☐No   ☐Sometimes

34) Do you think she is truthful?

☐Yes   ☐No   ☐Sometimes

35) Does she think that you are truthful?

☐Yes   ☐No   ☐Sometimes

36) Do you feel that you are able to be
yourself in the relationship?

☐Yes   ☐No   ☐Sometimes

37) **Do you feel like you permit** her to be herself
in the relationship?

☐Yes ☐No ☐Sometimes

38) **Do you feel heard?**

☐Yes ☐No ☐Sometimes

39) **Do you think** she feels heard?

☐Yes ☐No ☐Sometimes

40) **Do you make** eye contact while talking?

☐Yes ☐No ☐Sometimes

41) **Do you share** your feelings with her?

☐Yes ☐No ☐Sometimes

42) **Does she share** her feelings with you?

☐Yes ☐No ☐Sometimes

43) **As a couple, do** you have good communication?

☐Yes ☐No ☐Sometimes

44) **Do you feel** appreciated by her?

☐Yes ☐No ☐Sometimes

45) Do you think she feels appreciated by you?
☐Yes ☐No ☐Sometimes

46) Do you admire her for her accomplishments?
☐Yes ☐No ☐Sometimes

47) Does she admire your accomplishments?
☐Yes ☐No ☐Sometimes

48) Do you express affection toward each other?
☐Yes ☐No ☐Sometimes

49) Do you hold hands in public?
☐Yes ☐No ☐Sometimes

50) Do you help each other?
☐Yes ☐No ☐Sometimes

Smart Relationship Analysis
| *Quiz #2 Score*

Add up how many *Yes, No* and *Sometimes* answers you got.
Multiply each by the number of points indicated.
(*No* answers receive zero points.)

\# of *Yes* answers_________________ x 2 points = _______________

\# of *No* answers_________________ x 0 points = _____0_____

\# of *Sometimes* answers__________ x 1 point   =_______________

Total: ___________

YOUR SCORE	YOUR GRADE
90-10	Excellent
80-89	Good
50-79	Coping
30-49	At Risk
0-29	Failing

Couples' Quiz #3 for Women

Couples' Quiz #3 | *For Women*

1) At the end of your day, do you look forward to seeing him again?

   ☐Yes ☐No ☐Sometimes

2) Are you respectful toward him?

   ☐Yes ☐No ☐Sometimes

3) Do you feel respected by him?

   ☐Yes ☐No ☐Sometimes

4) Are you able to have a disagreement without cussing or yelling at each other?

   ☐Yes ☐No ☐Sometimes

5) Are you happy with him?

   ☐Yes ☐No ☐Sometimes

6) Are you able to have a conversation without ending up in an argument?

   ☐Yes ☐No ☐Sometimes

7) **Do you spend** alone time as a couple?
☐Yes ☐No ☐Sometimes

8) **Do you do special things to make him feel loved or appreciated?**
☐Yes ☐No ☐Sometimes

9) **Before starting** a conversation, do you take into **consideration** whether or not he is tired, hungry, stressed, unwell, or under the influence?
☐Yes ☐No ☐Sometimes

10) **Before reacting,** do you ask yourself whether or not you are tired, hungry, stressed, unwell, **PMSing,** or under the influence?
☐Yes ☐No ☐Sometimes

11) **Are you able** to work on your issues without **competing** over who is better or smarter, who is **right** or wrong?
☐Yes ☐No ☐Sometimes

12) **Do you work** as a team?
☐Yes ☐No ☐Sometimes

13) **In conversation,** are you able to stay on point **without bouncing** from topic to topic?
☐Yes ☐No ☐Sometimes

14) Are you able to have conversations without misunderstandings?

☐Yes ☐No ☐Sometimes

15) Does he use a good tone when speaking with you?

☐Yes ☐No ☐Sometimes

16) Do you think you use a good tone when speaking with him?

☐Yes ☐No ☐Sometimes

17) During conversations, do you feel understood?

☐Yes ☐No ☐Sometimes

18) Do you feel loved?

☐Yes ☐No ☐Sometimes

19) Does he make you feel special?

☐Yes ☐No ☐Sometimes

20) Do you think he feels loved by you?

☐Yes ☐No ☐Sometimes

21) Do you feel in love and as close as you used to be?

☐Yes ☐No ☐Sometimes

22) Do you stay away from TV, phone, and social media in order to spend time together?

☐Yes ☐No ☐Sometimes

23) Are you able to see the good in him without focusing on the negative?

☐Yes ☐No ☐Sometimes

24) Is he able to see the good in you without focusing on the negative?

☐Yes ☐No ☐Sometimes

25) Do you trust him?

☐Yes ☐No ☐Sometimes

26) Does he trust you?

☐Yes ☐No ☐Sometimes

27) Do you feel like you are getting the support you need from him?

☐Yes ☐No ☐Sometimes

28) Are you supportive of him?

☐Yes ☐No ☐Sometimes

29) Are you happy with your sex life?
☐Yes ☐No ☐Sometimes

30) Do you think he is happy with your sex life?
☐Yes ☐No ☐Sometimes

31) Do you feel that you are able to achieve
your goals within the relationship?
☐Yes ☐No ☐Sometimes

32) Do you feel that he is able to achieve
his goals within the relationship?
☐Yes ☐No ☐Sometimes

33) Do you work together on common goals?
☐Yes ☐No ☐Sometimes

34) Do you think he is truthful?
☐Yes ☐No ☐Sometimes

35) Does he think that you are truthful?
☐Yes ☐No ☐Sometimes

36) Do you feel that you are able to be
yourself in the relationship?
☐Yes ☐No ☐Sometimes

37) Do you feel like you permit him to be himself in the relationship?

☐Yes ☐No ☐Sometimes

38) Do you feel heard?

☐Yes ☐No ☐Sometimes

39) Do you think he feels heard?

☐Yes ☐No ☐Sometimes

40) Do you make eye contact while talking?

☐Yes ☐No ☐Sometimes

41) Do you share your feelings with him?

☐Yes ☐No ☐Sometimes

42) Does he share his feelings with you?

☐Yes ☐No ☐Sometimes

43) As a couple, do you have good communication?

☐Yes ☐No ☐Sometimes

44) Do you feel appreciated by him?

☐Yes ☐No ☐Sometimes

45) Do you think he feels appreciated by you?
☐Yes ☐No ☐Sometimes

46) Do you admire him for his accomplishments?
☐Yes ☐No ☐Sometimes

47) Does he admire your accomplishments?
☐Yes ☐No ☐Sometimes

48) Do you express affection toward each other?
☐Yes ☐No ☐Sometimes

49) Do you hold hands in public?
☐Yes ☐No ☐Sometimes

50) Do you help each other?
☐Yes ☐No ☐Sometimes

Smart Relationship Analysis
| *Quiz #3 Score*

Add up how many *Yes*, *No* and *Sometimes* answers you got.
Multiply each by the number of points indicated.
(*No* answers receive zero points.)

\# of *Yes* answers_________________ x 2 points = _______________

\# of *No* answers_________________ x 0 points = _____0_____

\# of *Sometimes* answers__________ x 1 point   =_______________

Total: _____________

YOUR SCORE	YOUR GRADE
90-10	Excellent
80-89	Good
50-79	Coping
30-49	At Risk
0-29	Failing

Couples' Quiz #3 for Men

Couples' Quiz #3 | *For Men*

Yes means yes or mostly.
No means no or rarely.

1) At the end of your day, do you look forward to seeing her again?

☐Yes ☐No ☐Sometimes

2) Are you respectful toward her?

☐Yes ☐No ☐Sometimes

3) Do you feel respected by her?

☐Yes ☐No ☐Sometimes

4) Are you able to have a disagreement without cussing or yelling at each other?

☐Yes ☐No ☐Sometimes

5) Are you happy with her?

☐Yes ☐No ☐Sometimes

6) Are you able to have a conversation without ending up in an argument?

☐Yes ☐No ☐Sometimes

7) Do you spend alone time as a couple?
☐Yes ☐No ☐Sometimes

8) Do you do special things to make her feel loved or appreciated?
☐Yes ☐No ☐Sometimes

9) Before starting a conversation, do you take into consideration whether or not she is tired, hungry, stressed, unwell, PMSing, or under the influence?
☐Yes ☐No ☐Sometimes

10) Before reacting, do you ask yourself whether or not you are tired, hungry, stressed, unwell, or under the influence?
☐Yes ☐No ☐Sometimes

11) Are you able to work on your issues without competing over who is better or smarter, who is right or wrong?
☐Yes ☐No ☐Sometimes

12) Do you work as a team?
☐Yes ☐No ☐Sometimes

13) In conversation, are you able to stay on point without bouncing from topic to topic?
☐Yes ☐No ☐Sometimes

14) Are you able to have conversations without misunderstandings?

☐Yes ☐No ☐Sometimes

15) Does she use a good tone when speaking with you?

☐Yes ☐No ☐Sometimes

16) Do you think you use a good tone when speaking with her?

☐Yes ☐No ☐Sometimes

17) During conversations, do you feel understood?

☐Yes ☐No ☐Sometimes

18) Do you feel loved?

☐Yes ☐No ☐Sometimes

19) Does she make you feel special?

☐Yes ☐No ☐Sometimes

20) Do you think she feels loved by you?

☐Yes ☐No ☐Sometimes

21) Do you feel in love and as close as you used to be?

☐Yes ☐No ☐Sometimes

22) Do you stay away from TV, phone, and social media in order to spend time together?

☐Yes ☐No ☐Sometimes

23) Are you able to see the good in her without focusing on the negative?

☐Yes ☐No ☐Sometimes

24) Is she able to see the good in you without focusing on the negative?

☐Yes ☐No ☐Sometimes

25) Do you trust her?

☐Yes ☐No ☐Sometimes

26) Does she trust you?

☐Yes ☐No ☐Sometimes

27) Do you feel like you are getting the support you need from her?

☐Yes ☐No ☐Sometimes

28) Are you supportive of her?

☐Yes ☐No ☐Sometimes

29) Are you happy with your sex life?
☐Yes ☐No ☐Sometimes

30) Do you think she is happy with your sex life?
☐Yes ☐No ☐Sometimes

31) Do you feel that you are able to achieve
your goals within the relationship?
☐Yes ☐No ☐Sometimes

32) Do you feel that she is able to achieve
her goals within the relationship?
☐Yes ☐No ☐Sometimes

33) Do you work together on common goals?
☐Yes ☐No ☐Sometimes

34) Do you think she is truthful?
☐Yes ☐No ☐Sometimes

35) Does she think that you are truthful?
☐Yes ☐No ☐Sometimes

36) Do you feel that you are able to be
yourself in the relationship?
☐Yes ☐No ☐Sometimes

37) Do you feel like you permit her to be herself in the relationship?

☐Yes ☐No ☐Sometimes

38) Do you feel heard?

☐Yes ☐No ☐Sometimes

39) Do you think she feels heard?

☐Yes ☐No ☐Sometimes

40) Do you make eye contact while talking?

☐Yes ☐No ☐Sometimes

41) Do you share your feelings with her?

☐Yes ☐No ☐Sometimes

42) Does she share her feelings with you?

☐Yes ☐No ☐Sometimes

43) As a couple, do you have good communication?

☐Yes ☐No ☐Sometimes

44) Do you feel appreciated by her?

☐Yes ☐No ☐Sometimes

45) Do you think she feels appreciated by you?
☐Yes ☐No ☐Sometimes

46) Do you admire her for her accomplishments?
☐Yes ☐No ☐Sometimes

47) Does she admire your accomplishments?
☐Yes ☐No ☐Sometimes

48) Do you express affection toward each other?
☐Yes ☐No ☐Sometimes

49) Do you hold hands in public?
☐Yes ☐No ☐Sometimes

50) Do you help each other?
☐Yes ☐No ☐Sometimes

Smart Relationship Analysis
| *Quiz #3 Score*

Add up how many *Yes*, *No* and *Sometimes* answers you got.
Multiply each by the number of points indicated.
(*No* answers receive zero points.)

\# of *Yes* answers_____________ x 2 points = __________

\# of *No* answers_____________ x 0 points = ____0____

\# of *Sometimes* answers________ x 1 point = _________

Total: _________

YOUR SCORE	YOUR GRADE
90-10	Excellent
80-89	Good
50-79	Coping
30-49	At Risk
0-29	Failing

Index

ADD/ADHD, 113-116

affection, 32-37, 88

alcohol, 7

assuming, 21

attitude, 50, 78

autism, 116

blended families, 101, 108

body language, 23

children, 101, 104, 106

communication:

    assuming, 21

    balancing, 85

    copy that, 124

    listening, 122

    twists and turns, 20

co-parenting, 101, 109

courtship, 36

criticism is toxic, 53

devices, curse called, 110

differences between you:

    drive, 89

    goals, 80

    messy, being, 91

    multitasking, 87

    racehorses vs. mules, 77

dishonesty, 57

disrespect, 56

escalation from conversation to fight, XII-XIII

"fighting correctly," XI—XII

garden of love, 31

grass is greener, 72

harmony, 77, 82

movies and TV, 46

positive, keeping it, 50

power struggle, 15

quality time, 102

respect 56

sex, 67

    foreplay, 68

    helicopters vs. airliners, 69

    how it deteriorates, 70

support, 60

team, 15-16

time, how you spend it, 49

timing, 5

tone, good/bad, 25

topic, bouncing off, 19-21

toxic influences, 43

    movies and TV, 46

    people, 44

    phones, 48

    social media, 47

truth, 59

www.ingramcontent.com/pod-product-compliance
Lightning Source LLC
Chambersburg PA
CBHW030917060726

47591CB00005B/1577